T0270520

SHINE THE LIGHT

SHINE THE LIGHT

HOW SANDLOT BASEBALL CONNECTS PEOPLE IN A DISCONNECTED WORLD

JIM MATTHEWS
FOREWORD BY ANNE R. KEENE

SPORTS
PUBLISHING

Sports Publishing books may be purchased in bulk at special discounts for
sales promotion, corporate gifts, fund-raising, or educational purposes. Special
editions can also be created to specifications. For details, contact the Special
Sales Department, Sports Publishing, 307 West 36th Street, 11th Floor, New
York, NY 10018 or sportspubbooks@skyhorsepublishing.com.

Sports Publishing® is a registered trademark of Skyhorse Publishing, Inc.®, a
Delaware corporation.

Visit our website at www.sportspubbooks.com.

10 9 8 7 6 5 4 3 2 1

Library of Congress Cataloging-in-Publication Data is available on file.

Jacket design by David Ter-Avanesyan
Front jacket photograph courtesy of Liz Matthews
Back jacket photograph courtesy of Alex Street

Print ISBN: 978-1-68358-492-6
Ebook ISBN: 978-1-68358-493-3

Printed in the United States of America

For my family. Thank you for always shining your light on me.

CONTENTS

FOREWORD

A Love Letter to Sandlot Baseball and Boyhood by Anne R. Keene

When I met Jim Matthews on the patio at Mozart's coffee shop overlooking Lake Austin, his eyes lit up when we talked about his mid-life return to baseball—sandlot baseball, a sport harkening back to the adolescence of our country in the 1870s.

Austin, Texas, is ground zero for the current sandlot revolution sweeping America.

Through the lens of Jim's book, you will come to understand how baseball, America's pure and simple game, is an elixir of youth, especially when it's played by grown men with aching joints and the weight of job responsibilities on a rustic baseball diamond.

Much of this book is set at the Long Time, a ballpark built on a floodplain with tin-roofed barns bordered by falling-over cedar posts—a pastural vista where Faulkner meets Austin cool.

As the Austin suburbs roar with construction, the Long Time magically connects players and fans with one thing they have in common: an innocent, old-fashioned childhood love of the game.

Sandlot baseball is portrayed in the motion picture film *The Sandlot. Sports Illustrated* shadowed the Texas Playboys, one of the flagship sandlot teams founded in the state of Texas. There's a podcast dedicated to the growth of this sport, but *Shine the Light* is the first narrative that takes readers behind the scenes of this grassroots institution that connects the generations and makes men feel like boys.

As an attorney and a former sportscaster, Jim has a conversational gift for storytelling that moves readers through the pages as he cycles through his early years in PONY League and the COLT League where his love of the game took root. We learn about his baseball journey through high school and college where he attempted to walk on the baseball team at the University of Texas, followed by a stint in "semi-pro" ball, where Jim thought he left the game for good after a final home run.

Behind the anchor desk at a television station, Jim realized that baseball worked to numb out family tragedy after the passing of his father, a pivotal event framing this book. As he looked back on his life, baseball proved to be the one true constant that never lost its hold, leading Jim to form a team called the Austin Moontowers in his mid-fifties.

As Jim journeys into the mythical world of baseball's past, you'll see modern-day sandlot ballparks with hand-painted wooden scoreboards and concession stands with affordable gourmet, Texas-style hot dogs. You'll see women toting YETI coolers or sometimes gloves of their own, both cheering for husbands and boyfriends or simply playing right alongside them. You'll meet the aging athletes spurring a revolution—grown men of muscle and sweat who were former high school and college players sidelined with injuries, as well as novices who've not touched a baseball in thirty years. In Austin, you'll meet the quirky sand-lot culture made up of artists, photographers, salesmen, professors, attorneys, and middle-aged athletes, along with a gamut of other professions. Players have handle-bar moustaches and beards. They wear weird mismatched socks, high tops, and retro-jerseys and ballcaps sold at ballparks to raise funds for charity, forging an identity and a sense of goodwill that goes along with this pastime.

You'll also meet the friends who inspired Jim's return to the game: Jack Sanders, the architect in his trademark Stetson who lit the fuse to the Texas sandlot movement twenty years ago and built the Long Time from the ground up; Howard Carey, a film producer and catcher at the helm of the digital #SandlotRevolution branding; and Elliott Hill, Jim's childhood friend and high school teammate, the Moontowers co-founder and person in lockstep with him as the two navigated the pitfalls of joining the burgeoning Austin baseball scene.

Shine the Light is a love letter to baseball and boyhood—an elegy about the power of the game that reawakens childhood memories with feel of the seams of a baseball, the crack of the bat, and the ceremonial gallop around the bases after a home run that can move a middle-aged man to tears because he realizes that home run might be his last.

I hope you enjoy this heartfelt journey into the sandlot culture as new teams emerge each year across the United States, Canada, and the UK. When actor James Earl Jones delivered his basso profundo "Build It, and They Will Come" monologue in the film *Field of Dreams*, he described the spirit of sandlot when he said, "This field, this game, it's part of our past. It reminds us of all that was once good." Sandlot baseball celebrates this bygone era of goodness, gifting baseball fans of all ages and backgrounds with an inclusive sport offering camaraderie, unbridled laughter, fresh country air, and child's play that's so desperately missing in society today.

AUTHOR'S NOTE

This story is a recollection of my memories. They might not be always be factually correct, but this how I remember it.

INTRODUCTION

We don't stop playing because we grow old. We grow old because we stop playing.

—George Bernard Shaw

I've loved baseball all my life and realized early on that any memoir I'd ever write would wrap itself around the game. But from my Little League years to a stint in a "semi-pro" league, nothing beats a special type of baseball—the sandlot variety.

To my utter embarrassment, I knew next to nothing about this peculiar old-school and extraordinary sport until much later in life, despite the fact that sandlot baseball is literally sweeping the nation and has been for years. Even after I "supposedly" gave up the sport for the umpteenth time, sandlot baseball reconnected me with my earliest baseball roots.

Honestly, I've lost track of the times I said, "Never again" to the hold baseball had (and has) on me, starting with college when I failed at a walk-on attempt. Even throughout several careers—TV personality, sports reporter, publicist, entrepreneur, and attorney—baseball followed me despite my on-again, off-again efforts to steer clear of its clutches.

SHINE THE LIGHT

Stumbling into sandlot baseball in my fifties changed my perspective of the sport forever. Sandlot is a different animal. The focus is about enjoying the sport with others—win, lose, or draw. A strong sense of *esprit de corps* and camaraderie exists without the cutthroat competition or pressure to win. Instead of me trying to make the All-Stars, impress a coach, or win a championship, it was now the collective experience of being among my pals, laughing and watching as we grow older together. Sharing this with my sons and watching my friends share it with their kids is all the reward needed.

That's the allure of the sandlot—a place for young and old alike to congregate, practice, and play. It's a place to let down your hair (if you have any left) and enjoy a break from everyday life while soaking up the great outdoors with others from your neighborhood, town, or even another city. Sandlot ballplayers can be complete amateurs, former high school players, semi-pros, or anything in between. They find themselves on scruffy fields and makeshift lots, playing their hearts out just like they did in childhood.

So, I've joined the sandlot movement—the enjoyment of community and a following of fans and friends I might not have otherwise met (many times, those who have heard about sandlot and just come out to see what it's all about). Some teams luck into playing in real venues, and others make a name for themselves outside of their states. My team, the Austin Moontowers Baseball Club, has had success locally playing teams in Austin and hopes to branch out soon. Running the team with an old friend is a labor of love, just like playing sandlot baseball is love personified for players of all stripes.

CHAPTER 1
THE PINNACLE

It ain't over till it's over.
—Yogi Berra

"No, man. You don't get it. I'm done," I said, almost jubilantly. I made a neck-slashing motion with both hands to emphasize the point. My teammate stared in disbelief as I took off my batting gloves and cleats, put my glove in my equipment bag, and strolled out of the dugout. I had just hit a home run, and my baseball career was over.

Well, "career" is being generous. Until then, baseball was the focal point of my life. From the time I was a four-year-old batboy through high school and college, I played baseball almost every day and dreamed about it when I wasn't on the field. It shaped me in small increments and provided the foundation for who I would ultimately become. Now, out of college, I was playing in a "semi-pro" game in San Luis Obispo, California, in 1993.

A real semi-pro team consists of college players who need a summer squad to keep their skills sharp. Semi-pro, in my case, meant former players who were out of college and still just wanted to toss the ball around. You probably know someone who says they used to play semi-pro. Chances are that was the highest level they had ever played when it wasn't even a level; it's just what we called it. Whatever the case, I was done. I was going out on top. While rounding the bases, I declared the home run the final at-bat of my life.

I was playing for the San Luis Obispo Blues at the time. With a young family and working as a sports anchor at KSBY-TV, the local NBC affiliate, nights and weekends were the busiest, so finding time to play baseball was usually a wasted exercise. I had two sons, and most days involved raising them or covering local athletic events for the sportscast that night. I was accustomed to being around ballplayers of all types, though, whether interviewing them or talking after a practice. One afternoon, after getting a sound bite from a local college coach, the discussion turned to whether I could still play. I had once been a decent player, reaching the college level, so with a certain cockiness, I said, "Sure, I can play." One thing led to another, and after a few phone calls, I became a member of the San Luis Obispo Blues. It was really just to prove that, yes, indeed, I still had it in me. Honestly, I saw it more as a disposable pursuit, a label I use without malice. But baseball and I had been drifting apart for a while, and I almost had it out of my system. Perhaps by playing on this team, I could depart my favorite sport in a blaze of glory and finally be done with it.

The Blues, founded in 1946, had been a long-running San Luis Obispo institution until the team folded in the 1980s. But visionary baseball aficionado Tim Golden had hopes of revitalizing it. For decades, semi-pro baseball had been a pastime in the towns along California's Central Coast. The Santa Maria Indians and Santa Barbara Foresters were popular and featured college players trying to stay in shape during the summers. Golden wanted to restore the Blues to what the team had once been when thousands would gather to watch them play. His vision would eventually pay off as the Blues today are the summer home for many college players and compete in the California Collegiate League.

Back then, though, the idea pitched to me was that he would spend a summer gauging community interest by putting a mix of players on the field to compete with whomever we could find. I'm not sure we were even called the Blues yet. We were there simply to have fun, build awareness, and reestablish the brand. In short, we were a bunch of guys hoping to have enough players to field a team any given weekend. Whoever showed up was whoever played. For me, playing baseball in the golden sunshine of California's Central Coast was a luxury I carved out of my busy schedule. I was so immersed in my home life and work that it rarely happened, so I had to make the most of my sparse appearances, especially when they let me hit in the leadoff spot.

During the years when I played regularly, I was a good hitter but not a home-run threat. I had a good eye and would rarely swing at pitches outside the strike zone. Although I hadn't played much recently, I knew I could at least get my bat on the ball. I usually hit in the leadoff spot and particularly loved hitting the first pitch. On the day of the home run, I was the first batter in the entire game, so when the pitcher's initial offering was a waist-high fastball, my eyes lit up, and I swung completely and through the ball. They say when you hit a baseball pure, you won't even feel the connection between the ball and bat, which is exactly what I remember.

The ball lofted high into the sun-splashed sky and began the unmistakable arc that could mean only one thing. It was headed far beyond the outfield wall. I saw the center fielder pivot, then lurch into a discombobulated turn, and it was obvious he would never reach it. The ball seemed to hang in the sky forever, and when it finally dropped beyond the center-field fence, I knew instantly this would be my last moment on a baseball field. I couldn't believe it. I was like Ted Williams, "Teddy Ballgame," "the Splendid Splinter," who had famously homered in his final at-bat for the Boston Red Sox.

I had reached the zenith. I could tell this story forever; nothing would come between me and this triumph. A smile crossed my face as I rounded second, and as I rounded third, I gave the base coach the obligatory handshake and then made my way for home. Knowing this would be my final moment in a lifetime dominated by the game, I eased up and looked around. Everything seemed to take on a white glow, like I was entering a baseball afterlife. The game had given me a lot, and I was ending my playing days the way everyone wanted to finish theirs, with a final moment of glory. I felt complete and whole.

I touched the plate and moved through the line of players offering me high fives until I reached the dugout. None of my teammates knew what I had in mind, but I went to the far end of the bench, sat down, peeled off my batting gloves, and then reached for my spikes. As I untied the laces, a teammate asked, "What are you doing?"

I said, "I'm done."

He said, "What do you mean you're done? The game just started."

I replied, "No, man. You don't get it. I'm done." And then I packed everything up and walked out of the dugout, leaving my baseball life behind me.

How was I to know that nearly thirty years later, it would start up all over again.

CHAPTER 2

DOESN'T THAT LOOK LIKE FUN?

Baseball is a universal language. Catch the ball, throw the ball, hit the ball.

—Pete Rose

I'm not sure exactly how it happened. Maybe it came about during an offhanded conversation, or I asked him a direct question. The details are fuzzy, but I do remember the subject very clearly. It caught me off guard, as baseball was once an almost daily ritual that had now laid dormant for nearly three decades. It was in 2019, the pre-COVID era, which, sadly, is the new line of demarcation in our lifetimes. I remember it was pre-COVID because even though we had the discussion, nothing came of it for more than a year until we were in the pandemic. This is how it began.

My childhood friend, Elliott Hill, was about to retire after thirty-two years of employment at Nike. He rose from a rank-and-file sales guy to becoming the company president and was being considered for the next CEO. But at some point, he needed to retire from the daily grind of a large multinational corporation and move back to his hometown of Austin, Texas, where we had grown up together in the 1970s and '80s. Our mothers had worked at the local high school, Reagan High, so we had known each other since we were barely five years old. They would take us, along with my older brother, Mark, and Elliott's older sister, Julia, to the school's Friday night football games to cheer from the bleachers with everyone else in our part of town.

Watching high school football was, and still is, a tribal custom in Texas and particularly in University Hills, our neighborhood in Northeast Austin. If you're not from Texas, the *Friday Night Lights* TV series (2006–11) gives a pretty good approximation of this culture. Adrenaline, extreme team loyalty, concession stands, mascots, marching bands, cheerleaders, and players—it shapes communities through love of the game.

University Hills was the suburban poster child of social and economic transformation. Affordable housing, good schools, and activities brought families of all backgrounds together. Athletics was the primary engine to generate cohesion among us kids, who ultimately became lifelong friends. Sports satisfied the collective longing for community most people sought, and still seek. And we were no different.

But it wasn't football that fascinated Elliott and me—it was baseball. Every day was designed around baseball, whether a game or a practice or simply tossing the ball in the front yard. Elliott was a little older than me, yet we were close enough in age to play baseball together at the nearby parks with the dozens of boys and girls we grew up with. We went to the same elementary school, and although I later moved to a different part of the city, it was still in the same district. By the time high school rolled around, we were back together at Reagan, where we played baseball on the JV and the varsity teams. He played first base and I played second.

After high school, Elliott went to TCU and then pursued a master's degree at the University of Ohio. I went to the University of Texas and studied journalism. During college, mutual child-hood buddies often traveled back and forth between Austin and Fort Worth, where TCU was located, so we kept in touch. Before the days of cell phones and texting, once someone moved away, it was difficult to remain friends. But since Elliott's mother lived in Austin, he visited often. All of us caught up, played golf, and enjoyed nights out.

After our careers began to wind down and our families were grown, it was time to rethink how the later years of our lives would play out. Elliott's work had taken him around the world, and I had left Austin at one point but returned seven years later to stay. So, it wasn't unusual for us, in 2019, to have dinner with our families or grab a beer with some of our pals, especially as Elliott was preparing for the move home.

Maybe it was during a Christmas visit or while he was scouting real estate, but somehow, we debated the next chapter of his life. How would he fill his newfound free time once he retired? We talked about various possibilities, and then, he asked, out of the blue, "Squidly-Dee, what do you think about playing baseball?" Squidly-Dee was his usual name for me, where it came from, I don't remember, but I had become accustomed to it. He paused for a moment and took a sip of his beer. "I think I might like to play again, just like when we were kids! Wouldn't that be great?"

Wait, what? Baseball? I had resolved never to play again. My life in baseball ended, even if it was among the lower forms in "semi-pro," triumphantly with that last home run. I was Ted

Williams or Michael Phelps, retiring on top! Nobody wanted to be Johnny Unitas in black high-top cleats with the Chargers, trying to resurrect glory that had long gone away. No way was I going back to that.

"Baseball, huh?" I asked, trying to seem interested. I was on the verge of relaying my story about how the home run had ended my career in triumph when he pulled out his phone and started to scroll through it.

"Yeah, baseball. I found a league that looks awesome. Take a look at this video," he enthused and pulled up what looked to be a short movie. And that was the moment when everything changed.

I didn't realize it at the time but I was watching was a video produced by YETI, the Austin-based drink mug/outdoors company that had grown into a national, if not worldwide, phenomenon. The video wasn't about their products. It was about baseball, particularly sandlot baseball, a league I had never heard about.

The video was about a team in Austin, the Texas Playboys, that I had also never heard about. And I was embarrassed. I was a baseball guy who had lived and breathed the game since I was born, growing up to become a professional sports anchor based solely on my love of the game. And there I was, with no clue about a baseball movement happening in my hometown. I continued to watch in awe.

The opening shot was a scratchy black-and-white image of a road, whetting my thirst for where it was leading me. Where would I go if I started down this path? This cowboy-professor-type guy appeared in front of a chalkboard with different words or what I thought were equations scrawled across it, almost daring me to discern what it meant. Then an older Black gentleman who had outgrown some of his teeth stood in front of words on the side of a building. "The Long Time," it said. What was that? Was it code for the undercurrent of baseball, a game where time is irrelevant?

The strange clues continued to draw me in when suddenly the cowboy-professor-guy reappeared on a ballfield, shaking hands with a ballplayer in the soft glow of a summer afternoon. I could feel the energy, the pull, and I knew something was happening. I wasn't sure what it was, but I knew I had once felt it. And so, I sat and let this unique story of baseball wash over me.

But this wasn't the type of baseball you might have heard of before. This was baseball being played in what appeared to be an imaginary place where anything was possible. And this video captured the essence of where my baseball dreams began, in the field across the street, in the backyard with my friends, and alongside the alleyway at my cousin's house. It was fielding ground balls for hours in the sweltering Texas sun, oblivious to anything else. It was pure and simple love of the sights, sounds, smells, and subtleties that make baseball special, the essence of the game. And here it was, unfolding in Austin.

For the next twenty minutes I sat, engrossed in the story of Jack Sanders and his team, the Texas Playboys (named after the Texas swing band of the same name), and how, ultimately, the sandlot league came into being. Sandlot baseball isn't the first or only league where men (and women) have played recreational baseball. Baseball leagues have launched throughout the country for several years, usually consisting of former high school, college, and some minor league players. I know about these leagues because former teammates have repeatedly asked me to play in them. But I always declined because I had given up the sport. I was through. Done. End of story—or so I thought.

I reveled in my account of going out on top. I liked to share that tale with friends, watching them gaze at me with a certain amount of admiration. *He did it his way,* their expressions seemed to say. *He didn't play one game too many and wind up in the emergency room.*

But here lay something different. Something unique. People who weren't gifted players were playing baseball for what appeared to be the joy of the game, on a sandlot, building a grassroots community through baseball. Men and women. Boys and girls. Dogs and roosters, and various other animals. They all dotted the fields with something in common—a desire to play a fun sport, despite cracks in the diamond, irregular basepaths, fences with holes, and gates with the rust of a thousand drops of rain. All these elements had called me to the game years before, and the old, familiar tug was happening once again.

As I watched, memories of throwing, running, hitting, and sliding stirred. It was something I instinctively wanted to be part of as it reached into the recesses of my soul.

In this league, the players might wear cowboy boots with their uniforms. Some played without uniforms at all. One player they interviewed described the feeling of going back to being a child. He said you could see it by the look in their eyes. Jack Sanders spoke about how baseball had become too corporate, where a hot dog costs nine dollars. The game had become out of reach for many people, except on the sandlot. This brand of baseball, for Jack and his Texas Playboys, had a purpose.

The video triggered something deep in my psyche, and I thought about how I perceived baseball while growing up. Old memories bubbled up. Baseball had been my life, and suddenly here was this video depicting everything I had once felt about the game but had apparently repressed when I became an adult.

When I was young, I listened to Astros and Rangers games deep into the night on a small radio tucked under my covers. As I drifted to sleep, I had visions of the Astrodome and beautifully manicured major league fields. But when I woke up and went out to play the game, we weren't in domed stadiums or on Astroturf; we were playing in the dirt lot at the end of the street or in a worn-down Little League field, with uniforms consisting of jeans and T-shirts. The baseballs were brown, as they were on the video. I saw players laying out the bases and raking the dirt before the games. It was the same game I knew so well, a game we played with the purest of hearts. It was the bad hops and stickers in the outfield grass all over again.

I watched the video in silence, and when it was over, I looked at my friend of more than fifty years. "Doesn't that look like fun?" he asked.

"Yes, it does," I agreed, no longer *trying* to seem interested. I was all in. The nostalgia took me to a different place where I was shaped and taught lessons, and rounded bases with graceful strides. And I could see it all coming back in a flash.

Elliott had grown up the same as me, had traveled on the same bumpy roads of adolescence, and felt the joy and sting of playing Little League, PONY, COLT, and finally, high school baseball. He knew what the sport meant and how it was perceived, enjoyed, and relished. And here he was, asking me if I wanted to experience those moments of youth all over again. At that exact moment, there was but one answer. Of course, I did!

There was only one problem.

I had no idea how to get involved, and neither did he.

CHAPTER 3
SQUID
————

Baseball gives a growing boy self-poise and self-reliance.
Baseball is a man-maker.

—Albert Goodwill Spalding

I don't remember the heat.

I guess it must've been hot, but how would I know? In 1976 I was wearing sweatpants under my uniform, trying to make my legs look more significant. I wore all sorts of things, arm bands, wrist bands, anything to make me look thicker than I was. I was skinny with a mustache when I was twelve. Think George Harrison during the Beatles' "White Album" era, and you'll get the idea.

I was so thin they called me Squid. It was some derivative of Squirt, the nickname I was stuck with after moving to a new neighborhood when I was ten. My family—Mom, Dad, and my older brother, Mark—had been living in Northeast Austin since I was four. When I was ten, we moved to a neighborhood called Oak Ridge near Braker Lane in far North Austin. Although the homes were fine, the surrounding area was less desirable. All around us seemed to be rows of low-slung cement buildings and an occasional metal shed. Across the street and behind our neighbors' houses was an area we called the Rat Flats. I thought it was meant for people who lived near creeks. I later learned it was a pejorative term.

My world centered around a two-block radius with plenty of kids to play with, and everyone had a nickname. Directly across from our house was Ricky Roo Rat. He was seventeen and worked at a junkyard. Greinert-The-Boy lived around the corner. Greinert always showed up at our home at five thirty when we were sitting down for dinner, and my dad would have no choice but to ask him to eat with us. He claimed Greinert's daily arrival time was so precise he could set his watch to it. A few houses away, on the other side of the street, lived "Gun." Before I moved there, his father had drunkenly come outside with a shotgun and brandished it about one night when the kids were shooting fireworks. My brother, even skinnier than I was, was aptly called "Bones." One day I went from being called Squirt to being called Squid. The older kids said it was something about me being all arms and legs. That was the entire story; nothing special except Squid is the name I still go by today. There was nothing better in 1976 than to be at bat in a Little League game and have some dad yell from the stands, "Come on, Squid!"

It wasn't my fault, though. My mom was a small Hispanic woman who never weighed over ninety pounds her entire life. My dad, Bobby, was six feet tall and the shortest person in his family. And that included his two sisters. Guess whose genes I got? My father's family was Scot-Irish, practical, and generally reserved. They came to America from England in the 1600s and settled in Virginia, where they were farmers by trade. But eventually, my grandfather Carl and his wife, Naomi, moved to a small town called Erwin, North Carolina, where he worked in a denim mill. That is where my dad, his brother, Leon, and two sisters, Geraldine and Daphine, grew up. They were no-nonsense people, and although financially stable, my dad quit high school to join the Air Force and earn money to help out. While stationed in San Antonio, he met my mother, Alice. Her family arrived in the United States from Saltillo, Mexico. My grandfather Pedro and his wife, Consuelo, ran a small grocery stand in San Antonio. There, in a small house near downtown, they raised my mother and her five siblings, Lupe, Rachel, Aurora, Susie, and Sammy, on turn-of-the-century values from south of the border.

I have always felt two competing bloodstreams flowing through me throughout my life. Both my parents were funny in their own right, and my sense of humor derived from their ability to see the lighter side of things. But, like most children of that era, they had experienced the aftermath of the Great Depression and World War II by the time they were eight years old, and much of the focus in our household was on education. They taught my brother, Mark, and me that effort and resilience were the cornerstones of any success we might achieve. It was how life was back in those days, especially where I grew up.

Many in the media would have you believe that the seventies-era Austin was dominated by musicians. But the city was filled with much more than the music scene. Austin, the capital of Texas, was filled with government officials, University of Texas employees, and a large group of military servicemen and women. Sprinkled among them were rough, rugged cowboys, as opposed to today's younger, more technology-focused population. Imagine lots of boots and belt buckles, cutoffs, and pickup trucks where we all rode in the back without a thought to safety. Johnny Cash and Charley Pride blared out of tape decks and eight-track players while neighbors washed their cars in their driveways on my street. There were no cell phones or video games to keep us indoors during the summers, and I moved among days of water hoses, lightning bugs, and sticky popsicles. The Austinites I knew worked diligently at their jobs and hobbies, often outside, in an unforgiving setting. I joined them under the glare of the Texas sun, with sweats on under my uniform.

Now, whoever said the bluest skies are in Texas must not have ever been there, at least during the summers when I was growing up. Texas summer skies are harsh and white, mainly due to a dull sheen of moisture that flows from the Gulf of Mexico, up I-35, through Austin, and toward the Dallas–Fort Worth metroplex. The water in the air seemed to settle in the sky and linger there, sometimes billowing up into huge storm clouds that dumped untold amounts of rain. Numerous games would get rained out, and many afternoons would be relegated to watching endless reruns of *The Beverly Hillbillies* or *Gilligan's Island*.

Yes, Austin is a rainy place. We get almost the same amount of rain the Pacific Northwest does, although ours seems to come in five or six downpours a year. But make no mistake, the summers in Texas are not for the faint of heart. They are for the ones who can overlook the heat, play ball in the dust and the mud, and are willing to put in the effort. For those of us determined to succeed no matter the cost, Texas made us harder, stronger, and more resilient.

And so, it was under the scorching heat and stark white light of the summer skies that I learned to love baseball. We played in the streets or the fields of a nearby elementary school. If none of the neighbor kids were around, I simply played by myself all day, making up games in front of my house. I imagine I was like most kids of that era, using some sort of ball to keep me entertained while I dreamed of bigger things beyond my extended neighborhood.

I threw a tennis ball against the wall in the road, where I fashioned a strike zone and pitched many a no-hitter in my head. If the ball hit off the bottom of the curb, it would pop into a fly ball, and I would catch it for an out. Sometimes I made it hit the curb in a certain way, and it shot over my head to the other side of the street—a home run. That always seemed to happen when I was the "other" team's pitcher. I played all day and into the evening. I played home run derby with my friends at the field at the end of the block. We made up games in San Antonio with my cousin and played "hotbox" with tennis balls in his backyard. Most of my enjoyable baseball time, though, was spent with my best friend, a guy named Greg Selber.

Selber was a good athlete and had this curly mop of hair that never seemed combed, which very few of us did growing up. He possessed a clatter of footspeed and agility but lacked focus. He constantly forgot things. I called him on the phone one day to go with us to a local waterslide. He told me to hold on while he went to ask his mom. He never returned to the phone, so we left without him. He said he waited for hours sitting on the curb with his towel. Then one night when we were older, he left his car running the entire night outside my house.

We called him "Sucker-Boy" due to his propensity to be gullible. We used to walk through the neighborhood, and I would read the names on the mailboxes and convince him that famous people lived there. It wasn't until he was almost sixteen that he finally began to wonder how both Richard Nixon and Tom Landry lived on the same street as me.

The unparalleled bond between us, though, was baseball. He and I would spend hours playing, discussing, and dissecting the sport. We loved the history, intrigue, and the stories of baseball legends. I guess we were junkies, devouring the sport however we could. We read the box scores every morning and *The Sporting News* on the weekend. When you were ten, you had to be a real baseball nerd to read *The Sporting News*. I watched Atlanta Braves baseball on the TBS Superstation back when it aired at two thirty in the morning, viewing through squiggly lines on the screen just before the explosion of cable TV.

I wore authentic MLB New Era hats long before they became ubiquitous. The only way to get one was to order it out of the back of *The Sporting News*, so I ordered a California Angels hat. I waited weeks for it to arrive and still remember the day it landed in the mail. I wore it to school the next day, and a friend asked if it was an actual MLB cap, as very few kids had seen one up close. A few weeks later, I left it on top of my mother's car, and she drove away. It was never to be seen again. I cried.

Selber, of course, bought an Oakland A's model from the lesser-known Roman Pro Cap company. It was ill-fitting and looked horrible on him, but he was proud to wear it. That's what we were, baseball people through and through. Perhaps it's why we both went on to have careers in sports. He was a newspaper sportswriter, and I became a television sports anchor. He later became a successful journalism professor in the Rio Grande Valley, authoring a couple of books about sports history along the Texas-Mexico border. For the time being, though, he was the only other person I knew who was as addicted to baseball as I was.

On the inevitable days when he was grounded and stuck in his house, we played Electric Baseball on the phone for hours. Anyone who has played Electric Baseball knows that you pull one lever to make the machine pitch and another to make the bat swing. I pitched and swung for both teams. Selber had to rely on me to tell him what was happening. Somehow, I always won.

Before I was a Little Leaguer, I loved the Cincinnati Reds, the Big Red Machine. I would run home from school to watch the MLB playoffs on television, which, back then, would be on weekday afternoons. I can still see Johnny Bench and Roberto Clemente standing in the gloam of the late afternoon at Riverfront Stadium when the Reds played the Pirates. But before then, there was nothing better than a fall Tuesday when the MLB playoffs were on TV. The Reds of that era were considered one of the greatest teams ever. I even bought a record with all my savings called . . . *And This One Belongs to the Reds!* It was an album with the Reds announcer Marty Brennaman, recalling all the best moments of the 1975 season.

I remember Pete Rose pummeling Mets shortstop Bud Harrelson in the '73 NLCS. My brother's hero was Bench, but mine was Rose. He was Charlie Hustle, Major League Baseball's all-time hits leader, who dove headfirst instead of sliding and ran to first on a walk (yes, I know about the gambling). Growing up, I was a smallish player who had to outhustle or outwork the other players to succeed, so I took my cues from Rose.

Have I mentioned that I never thought it was hot outside, not even in the dead of the Texas summer? Weird, I know. While others melted and wilted and occasionally passed out from the heat, I played no matter the temperature. And if I wasn't playing baseball in the sweltering climate, with sweat dampening my three-quarter-sleeve cotton shirts, I was thinking about it. I studied baseball even while everyone else went swimming or to the movies—the minutiae, daily and hourly. I craved the sound of the crack of the bat, the feel of sliding into second base, and the distinct smell of leather gloves. I wished the sun would never set and we could play forever.

My dad was blind in one eye, so he never participated in my sporting life. Despite not having a dad who played catch with me, I don't remember it being a handicap. He supported my interests and genuinely wanted me to be good, but he grew up without the luxury of sports. The focus was keeping food on the table and ensuring the children were educated. Playing games for entertainment wasn't something his family emphasized.

My mother's family, at least my aunts and uncles, all talked about sports and watched games when we visited with them during the holidays. I snuck into groups of my older cousins and uncles and sat quietly by, listening to their comments, absorbing the jargon, and picking up the more mature viewpoints of the game. But even as a young boy, I knew they were simply enjoying the games and not studying them the way I was. I was laser-focused on the fabric of baseball, and by the time I was twelve could talk with any grownup about the most obscure details of the game.

Like my mom, I was slightly built. So, what I lacked in size, I made up for with knowledge, relentless practice, and the hustle of Rose. I bought books to learn the game and went to high school and University of Texas games to see firsthand what I had absorbed. My apprenticeship in baseball came not as a player but rather when I was the batboy for my brother's team. He played at the Woodlawn Little League in San Antonio while my dad was finishing his military service at Lackland Air Force Base. My brother, Mark, is four years older than me and was my hero. He watched over me since I was the youngest kid on the block, consistently inserting myself into the games that he and his older friends played, usually a step behind and a little too slow.

Once, while he and his friends were playing in a field near our elementary school, I wandered away to explore a construction area and accidentally stepped on a rusty nail sticking out of a board. I remember Mark rushing over and scooping me up in his arms and running the blocks back to our house. His friends alternately tossed me back and forth between them as I grew heavier with each step. I recovered just fine but wonder what would've happened had he not been keeping an eye out for me.

Years later, I still remember when his foot slid underneath the lawn mower while cutting the grass, and he wound up losing two toes. I would've blacked out had that happened to me, but he never cried nor complained about what happened, and instead went back about his business once he healed. I ran all the way home from the bus stop the day he came home from the hospital. There he was, the expression on his face saying that he would do with eight toes what would take others ten.

I first became aware of the game watching my brother. He played baseball too and was a catcher. He was skinny like me but controlled the game from behind the plate, and I liked that. He seemed like the guy in charge. So naturally, catcher was where I wanted to be. But since I was only four years old, they wouldn't let me play, and I became the batboy. I didn't get to wear a uniform like the rest of the players. I had to wear shorts and a team cap.

One time someone got a hit, and I made a beeline toward the plate, knowing this was how I could get in the game. Unbeknownst to me, while I was retrieving the bat, a close play was happening, and I was now right in the middle of it. Everyone shrieked at me at once; the ump, the coaches, the players. Our coaches scrambled onto the field, and one lifted me out of the way just as the runner slid in. To the parents in the stands, I might as well have jumped in front of a car. They managed to pull me out just before certain death, but after that episode, I can't remember if I got fired or not, but I knew, even then, picking up the bats was not where I belonged. I needed to be on the field.

When I turned eight, I was old enough to play Little League. By then, we lived in Austin as my dad had retired from the Air Force, and our family settled in University Hills. All the kids in our neighborhood played at Delwood Northeast Optimist. But now that I was a player, I finally got to wear an actual uniform like the players I had grown up watching on TV, only to be heartbroken the day they were handed out. Since I was only in the "Farm" league, our uniforms consisted of blue jeans and a T-shirt with our team sponsor on the back. Only the "Major" league players could wear an official uniform, and I was mired down among the other eight-year-olds. And to make it just slightly worse, our teams were not named for big league clubs. We were named after our sponsors; thus, my team was called Hooker Auto Service. The following year wasn't much better. Even though I had moved up to the "Minor" league, I still had not reached the level required to wear a certified uniform. This time my team was called M. E. Gene Johnson, which, coincidentally enough, was also an auto repair service.

When I was ten, we moved to another part of town, and I played in the Walnut Creek Little League. Fortunately, our teams were not named for their sponsors in this league. Instead, we had actual major league teams, with names like the Astros and Cubs. Unfortunately, we also had teams named for football teams, and I was put on the Steelers. It wasn't a true baseball name, but at least we had uniforms.

During that era, which one could argue as the worst sartorial period in major league history, the Little League uniforms were modeled on those worn by big league teams in the mid-seventies. And they were simply hideous. They were the old double-knit polyester pullover jerseys with the Sansabelt pants. I had missed the golden era of the button-up jerseys with lovely piping on the front. Even when I got into high school, we still wore those polyester-style uniforms. Still, it was a uniform, and despite being only ten, I made it onto a major league team of eleven- and twelve-year-olds, which gave me the impression I was on my way to becoming a big leaguer. It didn't take long for reality to set me straight.

During the time I was playing at Walnut Creek, my brother got cut from the PONY League tryouts. This was back when only one team won a trophy, and some people didn't make the team. But my brother? He was the player I looked up to the most. I was so proud that he was older and a catcher. It left me devastated to hear he wasn't good enough to be a starter much less make the team. It was my first experience with disappointment in baseball, and I felt horrible for him. Soon, though, he gravitated to other sports like golf and swimming, for which he was better suited and could excel, and he did. Ultimately, he became a firefighter, spending his adult life rescuing others instead of me.

Meanwhile, I plowed ahead with baseball. It was all I knew back then and the only thing I cared about, especially making the All-Stars. At the end of every season, the coaches got together and decided which players had the best season. Then after the championship game, the names were called out in a big ceremony on the field, making up the All-Star team. If selected, you could continue playing in tournaments, advancing as far as the World Series of whatever league you were in, provided that you kept winning. After my eleven-year-old season, I was confident I was a candidate for the squad, so I went to the ceremony at the field and sat in the stands while they announced who had made the team.

One after another, the coaches who had been the champions that year (the champion coaching staff always became the All-Star coaches) called out fifteen names. Mine was not among them. But, as the disappointment enveloped my body like a cancer, they announced that three more names would be called. These would be the alternates, players to be added to the team if someone got hurt or was on vacation and couldn't play. This was to be my moment of triumph. And so, I waited for the new names to be called on the verge of delirium. I wanted it so desperately.

They announced two more names. Neither was mine. Then they got to the last name. Steve Sargologos, a teammate sitting next to me who also had hopes of making the team, grabbed me, and we embraced, like the finalists at a Miss America pageant, each wanting to hear our name called but keeping our emotions in check should it be the other. And finally, just as I could not take in another breath, my entire childhood resting on this moment, they called the final name.

It was neither me nor Steve. Instead, it was some kid who had played the season with a broken arm, and they were doing it to congratulate him on having a fine year. Steve and I let each other go and simply stared out at the field as everyone clapped and yelled encouraging things. I was destroyed. It was as if baseball had let me down, had broken up with me, and had said you aren't welcome anymore. My coach even came by my house the next day to console me while he told me how the vote went down. He said I came close and should've made it, but it didn't happen.

The coach was Val Gonzalez, and I remember him because we sat on my front porch while he broke the news to me. I always appreciated him for doing that as it made me understand, even at that early age, that sometimes things were out of my hands and, instead, it would be better to work on what I *could* control. And so that winter, I worked at the craft of baseball. Harder than I ever had. And by next season, I hit seven home runs and was the first player selected to the All-Star team when it was announced.

Things were great while we were in Little League, but the next year we would have to move into another league for thirteen- and fourteen-year-olds several miles from our home. We played with a bunch of guys we had never met from a different part of town, and a rumor spread about one guy, in particular, Joe Dunnigan. He was a legend in every neighborhood, and so big that he outgrew his uniform. Selber and I were scared to death of him, and we hadn't even seen him in person.

We prayed that we would make it onto Joe Dunnigan's team at tryouts. Yet, as luck would have it, our league decided not to hold tryouts that year. Instead, they took everyone who wanted to move into PONY baseball and stuck us on a team . . . something about a merger. I didn't know all the collective bargaining terms then, but one thing was for sure: Selber and I would be on a team together, and Joe Dunnigan would not. We were already doomed.

CHAPTER 4

STIR CRAZY

Playing baseball is not real life. It's a fantasy world. It's a dream come true.

—Dale Murphy

It had been nearly three decades since I had last been in a batter's box, but there I was, in the spring of 2021, walking to the plate for my first at-bat since the home run I hit in California. I knew my legs were moving closer to the plate and could feel the bat in my hands. It was a walk I had made a thousand times, yet this felt different as I settled into the box at Downs Field in East Austin. And as I looked out to the mound and glimpsed the first live pitcher to glower in at me in nearly thirty years, I realized this wasn't so different after all. In fact, it was all too familiar. And that is precisely when I could no longer feel my legs, hands, or the bat I held. It had suddenly become an out-of-body experience.

Only three weeks prior, I had been comfortably sitting at my desk in the guest house behind my home where I worked. This was where I had become accustomed, day after day, to interact with the world through a computer camera lens due to COVID-19. Remote work and remote meetings were the new way of doing business, even in the legal world. I missed dealing with judges, clients, and my fellow lawyers in person at the courthouse. Being cooped up and isolated took some getting used to.

It had been more than a year since Elliott and I talked about playing baseball with the Texas Playboys. When we initially discussed playing again, it seemed like such a perfect idea, as all ideas are until called to action. But I knew better. I knew it would only lead to heartbreak. And who was I to kid? In my mind, I would be on a well-groomed field of green grass, scooping up grounders, hitting balls into the gap, and flying around the bases. But after careful contemplation, I knew the truth. I wouldn't be flying around the bases. I would hobble. I wouldn't be fielding grounders. I would play them off my shin. I wouldn't be ringing doubles into the alley. I would tear a ligament trying to swing the bat.

But now, with COVID becoming less of a threat, I was confused, disoriented, and aching to get out of the house. Along with everyone else, I had been in a deep freeze while it ravaged the world around me. I was spared, but so many others had not been as fortunate. I knew many people who lost someone to the disease. My own mother, who suffered from dementia and lived alone in an assisted living facility, probably had no idea why her son wasn't allowed to see her, or why everyone was wearing strange masks. With this idea in my head, days could no longer be taken for granted.

Even when things were getting somewhat back to normal, the threat of being shut in again always lurked. It made me want to get outside, do exciting things, and experience life as it was meant to be. In person, up close, and with other people. Perhaps it was the right time to play baseball again? Or at least think more about it. So, I called Elliott.

"Hey, man," I said after we had gone through the usual pleasantries of the phone call (a custom that is fading in our lifetime, unfortunately). "You remember that baseball thing we were talking about a year ago? The video you showed me? You, uh, you still interested in that?"

"Aww, Squidly-Dee," he responded in a Texas drawl halfway between humility and assuredness. "You know me. I'm busy and real tired. But heck, yeah, let's do it. It'd be fun. Don't you think?"

"Uh . . . " I paused. I was surprised. I had hoped he would say something like, no, he was busy (which he said) and too tired (which he also said) but that maybe it was something that we should think about and not rush into just yet. But he didn't say that. He said quite the opposite, and now I was on the spot, suddenly overcome again with all the thoughts of what could go wrong.

"Yeah, I do," my voice grew fainter. I wasn't sure if I really wanted this or not. "Right?" I added. But I knew this was the moment. There was no going back now.

"Good. It'll be fun. Did you find the Playboys?"

I hadn't found them. I hadn't even called them. I hadn't done anything with the idea since we had last talked about it more than a year before. I still didn't know who the Playboys were or how to get in touch with them, and I knew nothing other than they seemed to be this interesting baseball team with an incredible field somewhere east of town.

"Uh . . . well, no." At least I was honest. "I haven't called anyone, and I didn't want to start nosing around until we had talked about it."

"Well, call them, and let's go. I want to get back to doing things instead of sitting behind my computer all day." He was used to getting things done and getting them done quickly.

"You and me both. Except, well, I haven't thrown . . . I haven't . . ."

"Stop sounding like an old man," he cut me off. Elliott had many charming traits, and positivity was perhaps his greatest asset. I, however, was constantly rooted in caution. This might have something to do with law school, which I pursued after my career in sports news. Lawyers are trained to be careful, so throwing caution to the wind and putting myself on the spot was uncomfortable.

Besides, I had ended my career on top with a glorious home run and a triumphant trip around the bases. Why would I want to come back now? To show off? What was I going to show? I could barely run down the street without popping a knee out of alignment. To prove to myself that I could still do it? Not only that, I had no idea how to get ahold of anyone, much less the Playboys.

"Awww, Squidly-Dee, listen," he paused. "We gotta keep the old man out," he added. "Look, playing baseball is what we did as kids. It was fun then. Why wouldn't it be fun now? What's to stop us from doing it again?"

I guess the answer to that was, really . . . nothing. Actually, there was everything, but at the moment, that particular *moment*, my mind went blank. For a split second, I sat there, unable to speak, but after hearing the excitement in his voice, my thoughts reverted to the devastation of being shut in by COVID, so I made my decision.

"Okay. Let me check around."

"All right then. Just let me know. Tell me when you want to throw," and he hung up.

Now, little did I know that the league the Playboys played in, the Sandlot League, wasn't the only league in town. There were several leagues. They were all over the place—the Central Texas League, the something else league, apparently a Mexican league. I had no idea where to start, so I started browsing online, at which point I stumbled across something that at least sounded like a place to start. It was called the Austin Metro Baseball League. They played at a tremendous historic ballpark, Downs Field, deep in East Austin.

I had played there back in the day, and as I recall, it was top-notch. If nothing else, it had a roof over the bleachers, creating a small stadium effect. Plus, the league had a website and what looked to be a commissioner. Perhaps, I thought, maybe if I showed interest in his league, we might get to talking, and then the commissioner could tell me how to get in touch with the Playboys. I dialed the number.

"Metro Baseball League, Mark speaking." (Wow, that was easy.)

"Uh, yeah . . . Hi, my name is Jim Matthews. And I'm wondering, uh, how, well, you see, I'm over fifty and was wondering . . ."

"You wanna play in the over-fifty league? Sure. Let me get your number, and I'll have one of the coaches contact you."

"Well, no, see . . ."

"How many you got?"

"What?"

"How many of you want to play?"

"Well, see, there's another guy and me." I knew I was only trying to answer his question. If he had given me just a second more, I would've explained that we were only *thinking* about playing, but it was too late.

"Perfect. I have a team looking for a couple of guys. What's your number?"

I gave him my number, and he hung up. Hmm. I wasn't sure what had just happened, but at least I had dialed the phone and put the idea into the universe, giving me another reason to believe it was the right thing to do. I could at least now be comfortable letting Elliott know I had contacted someone and we could just sort of slow-play things—maybe throw a little, take some batting practice together, and maybe by next year, be in shape to play somewhere.

Suddenly, my phone rang. I didn't recognize the number, but picked up anyway.

"Hello."

"Hey Jim, this is Chris Hux with the Express in the Austin Metro Baseball League. Heard you were looking to play some ball."

What? It had been two minutes.

"Uh, yeah. Me and another guy." (I wasn't getting involved in this by myself.)

"Great, listen, we are just getting this season started. We open our season in a couple of weeks, but we have batting practice next Wednesday. I'll shoot you a text with the address."

"Uh . . . okay, yeah, that sounds fine."

"Okay, perfect. See you then," and then the line went dead.

I wasn't even finished. I wanted to ask more questions and let him know we needed time to think about things. But he had hung up. A half hour ago, I had sat contemplating whether to bring up the baseball idea with Elliott, and now here I was (or

instead, we were) somehow on a team. And we had batting practice in less than a week. And now I had to call Elliott back and
deliver the news, which I wasn't sure was good or not.

"Hey, man," I said, trying to sound calmer than I was since it
was only ten minutes after we had last talked. "Yeah, you're not,
uh, not gonna believe this, but I think I got us on a team."

"Playboys?"

"Well, not exactly. I found this over-fifty league. I called the
guy, and they were looking for a couple of players. They may
have batting practice coming up soon. I'm not sure yet (I lied),
but if they have it, they said we could go by and see if we want
to join. So, I thought we might throw a little, hit a few balls, and
maybe check out the batting practice. That is if they have it."

Long silence.

"What happened to the Playboys?"

"Well, that's still in the works. (I lied again.) "But," I said, trying to change the subject, "why don't we just get out and throw a
little and hit a few, and maybe if they call back, we can be ready?"
I was now asking for his validation of my awful mistake, which
he didn't even know I had made.

"All right, let me look at my schedule."

I wasn't sure if I was relieved or excited, but at least being on
the Playboys and my inability to get past that first step was no
longer the issue. The focal point had now become whether we
could hit a baseball again.

Two days later, I drove Elliott to a warehouse area south of Ben
White Boulevard. If you have ever been to Austin, you'd know
this is not one of the more deluxe areas of town. It is more suited
to a propane tank explosion than a business. But tucked back
among various warehouses and an occasional strip bar, there was

a metal building with a batting cage inside. We walked in and could immediately tell by the sizes of bats and helmets for rent that it was geared toward ten-year-olds, not the former president of Nike and his high school pal.

We had no helmet, no bat, and no choice but to rent them if we wanted to get into a cage with a pitching machine. The machine was problematic as neither of us could figure out how to work it, but we were ready to go once we brought the manager/ninth grader over to help. I hit first, and we set the machine on fifty miles per hour. At first, it was difficult even to grip the bat as I had developed arthritis in my right wrist over the years and didn't realize how much pain that movement would bring me. I managed to eke out a couple of ground balls when suddenly I heard Elliott's unmistakable drawl behind me.

"All right, boys, here is Squidly-Dee, showing us how he can hit. In the cage, our first day back at it as we get ready to play in a—oh wow, nice shot, Squid—an old man's baseball league."

I finally hit one that reached the pitching machine.

"Nice cut! Did you boys see that?"

I then realized he wasn't talking to me, but instead, he was taking a video to send to our old high school friends. Before I could even get out of the cage to stop him, he had already pressed the send button.

"Boys are gonna love this," he declared. There was nothing I could do about it, plus I was more concerned about a weird sensation in my knee that had joined the pain I felt in my wrist.

Elliott stepped in, so I grabbed my phone and began shooting videos of him. He took a few basic cuts, which went back and forth for a while, both of us hitting a few weak ground balls. Sometimes we managed a line drive of sorts. After two rounds, we realized there were only so many swings inside of us, so we left the batting cage and went outside to play catch. As I mentioned, we were smack in the middle of several warehouses with miles of chain link fences topped by barbed wire everywhere. There were no curbs on these streets; just empty storm drains with weeds growing up to our shins. We found an area underneath some electrical wires and casually tossed the ball around.

After a few throws, I stopped lobbing and tried to cut loose with one, which didn't go so well. The ball wound up in the ditch off to the side. To make matters worse, I realized we could only throw the ball a certain distance, which didn't seem very far. A quick calculation in my head left me to estimate each throw was on a line for only about thirty feet before beginning its descent. We were catching every one of them around our ankles.

Even after becoming loose, the throws didn't seem to improve, so we took a break to discuss our concerns. We decided to walk off what we thought was ninety feet, the distance between the bases and a distance we could have threaded a proverbial needle on every throw when we were in school. When I looked at Elliott standing those ninety feet away, it might as well have been the Grand Canyon. I took a large gulp and then tried to throw it to him. It got there but was really more of a pop fly, as high as it was far. Things were going horribly wrong, and I could feel it. My wrist didn't allow me to finish my motion, and my knee felt weird, so that I couldn't push off with my leg. I was basically shot-putting the ball to him.

"Hey man, how's your arm feeling? Mine is hurting," he yelled.

"I think we've done enough damage for the day," I responded happily, knowing the nightmare was over. We got back in the car, but once we reached his house, the aches and pains had subsided just enough that we convinced each other that our former glory wouldn't be that hard to reach if we simply applied ourselves. So, it was agreed we would go to the team batting practice the next week and see what might unfold.

The following Wednesday, we arrived together at an indoor batting cage in the back of a machine shop on Burnet Road in the middle of town amongst assorted used car dealers and self-storage units. As we walked in, every face was trained on us with the same unmistakable expressions that said, "Who in the world are you?"

"Uh, hey guys, I'm Jim Matthews." Long pause, no response. "I was told to show up here for practice."

"Hi, I'm Elliott." Even longer pause, still no response. "You boys look serious."

It was as if we were from Mars. No one could figure out who we were or why we were there. I later learned I had inadvertently gotten us tangled up in perhaps the top men's league in Central Texas and on what was probably the best team. The league was for players anywhere from eighteen years to a division of over sixty. They were primarily former ballplayers who were good in high school, college, and perhaps the minor leagues. Many had not stopped playing since their earlier days. The Express were in the over-fifty division, which I discovered later, had played together since the late eighties. We noticed several trophies in a case depicting them as state champs in one age group after another, so I guess they weren't too keen on just anyone trying to become part of their esteemed legacy.

After an eternity, one of them finally offered up his hand, told us they were glad to meet us, and asked if we wanted to jump in the cage. I was already feeling something weird in my knee, and I know Elliott had barely swung the bat in at least four decades, so it was with great trepidation I agreed. That fear turned into horror when I realized we weren't going to take cuts off a machine. An actual guy was throwing from behind a net, and by the looks of things, he was probably a former college pitcher. He was 6-foot-4 and mixed in curves with fastballs. After seeing a hitter miss the last pitch by about two feet, I knew he was also changing speeds.

"Yeah, Elliott, why don't you jump in? Let me, uh, loosen up," I said uneasily. My sense of concern was compounded by my distress. His only response was, "All right," with what sounded like some measure of confidence. But before he jumped in the cage, he pulled me aside. "Squid, I'm nervous. I don't get nervous about anything, but somehow I'm nervous." So was I. But he couldn't tell because I had already turned and walked as far away from him as I could. I couldn't bear to look.

The person on the mound had clearly been, at the very least, a former college pitcher who, after one glance at us, could sense our feebleness and, in a show of grace, threw about half speed and no junk. After a few swings, Elliott got ahold of a couple of grooved fastballs and soon sprayed line drives rattling around the far end of the cage. Then it was my turn to step in, and I guess the adrenaline masked the pain in my knee. After a couple of swings, something clicked in, and I could sense my swing resembling something I had done several decades before. After a few minutes, we could time our swings enough to send a few shots back the other way. Soon it seemed more or less familiar and more or less like baseball.

We wound up jumping in and out with the other guys, and although we were light years behind them, at least we weren't embarrassing ourselves. That is until I stood near whom I perceived as one of the assistant coaches. The head coach, who called me the week before, hadn't arrived yet, so it was not surprising that the other players had no idea who we were. I could hear the assistant on the phone, though.

"Well, they seem okay (long pause). No. (He glanced over at us, then quickly looked away.) No, I haven't seen them throw yet."

At the end of the workout, Elliott and I stood around talking with the players, all of whom appeared to be in their late fifties and early sixties. They each possessed an athletic build that said they had kept active, although a few showed the wear and tear a constant life of baseball could take on a body. There were assorted taped fingers and knees wrapped, and a couple walked with a noticeable limp. For the heads with hair, the gray blended with the white giving them the look of an umpire more than a player. But in the end, they became friendly and soon loosened up the way ballplayers do in these settings.

"Where did you play?"

"Oh yeah?"

"You know so and so?"

"Yeah, my hip has been acting up too, but I still like to get out and play a few games a year."

After a few discussions about when the following practices were and where the games would be, I could tell Elliott wasn't that enthused, so we left. On the way to the car, he said, "Squid, there is no way I can play that many games. He showed me his phone. "Look at my schedule. I'm gonna be gone most of the summer in Oregon, and then we go to our place in Italy."

"Well, just play as many games as you can. It doesn't look like they will be counting on us to carry the team. We can work ourselves back into shape and then maybe hook on with the Playboys next year."

"Yeah, about them," he asked again. "Whatever happened to that?" Dang. I shouldn't have brought it up. "You know," he went on, "I don't think this is the same thing we saw on the video. The guys in the video looked like they were having fun. They seemed to be all smiles and had a great sense of community. These guys looked like they were serious."

He paused. I could tell something important was coming. "Squid, I wanna play with guys I know and guys I feel comfortable having a beer with. I'm not sure this is what I'm looking for." Quite honestly, I wasn't sure myself, but I still had no idea how to get ahold of the Playboys, and I figured with this team, we could at least take some batting practice.

"What about getting some BP in with these guys and playing one or two games?" I replied. By now, he was back on his phone, and I could sense by his lack of a response he had already made up his mind. He confirmed that feeling when he called the next day and told me he was out. He wasn't going to play. He would hold out for the Playboys, but he wasn't going to play in this league. I told him I understood and wished I had made the same decision. I didn't have the heart to tell him that a few minutes after the previous night's practice, the coach had called to apologize for being late and was sorry he didn't have a chance to meet me in person, but he was looking forward to meeting me at our first game. There was a fleeting moment when I could've gotten out, but I panicked and simply said it would be great to meet him and asked him when I needed to be there at the game. Which I found out was to be ten days later.

So that is how I wound up at Downs Field in East Austin on a warm spring afternoon, playing with the Austin Express in the over-fifty division of the Austin Metro Baseball League. I arrived after the over-sixty team played in the game before us and stood near their dugout as our guys were piling in. I could hear the coach yelling at his players, "We gotta hustle! We gotta get down on those grounders! We gotta check the third-base coach for the signals!!"

One player yelled, "Hey man, I don't need this. I can barely see down to third base anyway."

I was sure this was some cruel joke I was playing on myself, but soon more of my teammates arrived, and eventually, the scene took shape. I was going to play in a baseball game for the first time since the early nineties, and as I warmed up in the outfield, it all felt familiar again. Once the game started, the old sounds and smells, and rhythms of the game came back as if I had never been away. I enjoyed sitting on the bench with the rest of the players, engaging in the usual dugout banter, until the fifth inning when the other team made a pitching change.

"Matthews, grab a bat," my coach bellowed out.

Suddenly, everything took on a dreamlike quality and began to move in slow motion. My son and his girlfriend were visiting from Denver, and I could see them crane their necks as I emerged from the dugout. My other son was also there, preparing for the Texas Bar Exam and taking time out of his badly needed studying. He put his book down as he turned his head toward me, like the guy opening his umbrella in the Zapruder film. Out of the corner of my eye, I also saw my wife, Liz, to whom I have been married for over twenty years. She was about to laugh or cry. I couldn't tell which.

I could hear their voices straining to offer words of encouragement. "Let's go, Papa," they yelled, although their words seemed faint as if coming from a distance. Elliott was there also, with his wife, Gina. They had biked over for the occasion and had joined my family in the stands, lapping up the sunshine while Elliott enjoyed the freedom he had manufactured by getting out when he had the chance. "Come on, Squid," they yelled. "You can do it!"

I could sense them all looking at me with a mixture of pride and morbid curiosity. I put on the new helmet I bought at Dick's Sporting Goods two days before and grabbed my wooden bat, part of the same purchase. Thankfully I had remembered to put pine tar on it, or it would have flown out of my hands as my swing resembled anything but that of an experienced player. My nerves were overflowing. But, undaunted, I strode to the plate and stepped in. I waved my bat back and forth as I had done thousands of times before and stared out at the mound. And suddenly, I knew why I could no longer feel my hands and legs. Glaring back at me from sixty feet, six inches away, was none other than Joe FREAKING Dunnigan.

Chapter 5

BALL FOUR

More than any other American sport, baseball creates the magnetic, addictive illusion that it can almost be understood.

—Thomas Boswell

Joe Dunnigan was the most feared pitcher in all University Hills Optimist back in 1978, which meant he was among the most feared pitchers in all of Austin, which was no small feat. In the late seventies, Austin wasn't a small town like many say; it was already a medium-sized city with over three hundred thousand people. And now, playing baseball at University Hills Optimist meant playing games in a new part of town rather than in my comfortable neighborhood with the park down the street. Gone would be the days of home runs over a fence 200 feet away. Now we would play in a big park where it was 315 feet to left field, 352 feet to center, and 300 to right.

More importantly, I was no longer one of the better players in the league. I was lumped in with guys older and much bigger than me, and it seemed like everyone else was growing sideways while I only lengthened out. There was no muscle to be found anywhere on my body—only the mustache.

Along with Delwood Northeast, University Hills Optimist, or UHO, was the most challenging place to play baseball in the entire city. The players in those leagues were from middle-class families where athletics, often more than education, meant the quickest way to a brighter future. They were all power, forged in the crucible of competition unlike anyplace else in town. They played with a swagger that told everyone that, for them, baseball was more than a game; it was a way of life. Some were already sixteen years old and wore metal spikes. A few even *drove* themselves to the games. I still remember my friend Adam Ortega and his older brother, Anthony, zooming into Reznicek Field, their Pinto on two wheels. Their hands waved as music blasted from the stereo, trying to right the car as it careened across the gravel parking lot.

This was a whole new world for Selber and me. We were just two blundering kids, barely thirteen, and we would now play PONY and COLT baseball for the next four years in this high-profile league miles away from our Little League. PONY League was for thirteen- and fourteen-year-olds, and COLT for fifteen and sixteen. UHO had just sent a team to the COLT League World Series, and it was widely known if you wanted to prove yourself, you needed to play at either UHO or Delwood. It was both an exciting and frightening prospect to play baseball at UHO, especially with a player of Joe Dunnigan's caliber in the mix.

Before tryouts that year, parents and coaches from our Little League got together and decided since UHO was so far away, it would be better if we consolidated into one team and practiced closer to our original neighborhoods. It wasn't up to the kids, but the parents, so they agreed to create one team from our old league. That's how Selber and I wound up on something called Climate Engineering. Instead of drafting a squad through try-outs, our team was put together from the names of players who simply signed up. As if assembled from a scrap heap, it was a team of castoffs and misfits, the biggest of which were Selber and me. And why wouldn't we be? We had to face a league of players older than us, among whom was a name we had only heard about but had never seen until one day, we went to the ballpark to watch some of the teams play.

The first time I laid eyes on Dunnigan, I was horrified. He was already a grown man. He was bigger than every player in the league and most coaches, too, like a Texas Paul Bunyan. His team wore breathtaking button-up, gray, wool uniforms with all the lettering and numbers stitched on, like the '27 Yankees. But just as had been advertised, Dunnigan wore polyester and all-white pants.

Mike Conroy was one of my good friends and their third baseman, and when I asked why Dunnigan's pants were not the gray wool like everyone else's, he responded with glee, "Because none of 'em would fit him." It was true. He had outgrown his uniform, as we had been hearing for the last year. I was mortified, and Selber was of no help. He was as alarmed as I was. And to make matters worse, he and I had recently discovered the book *Ball Four*.

Selber and I both loved to read, especially books about baseball. We spent hours devouring books like Roger Angell's *The Summer Game* and *Five Seasons*. Also, Roger Kahn's *The Boys of Summer*. We didn't know anyone else our age (or anyone else, quite honestly) who read stuff like this. We found our books at various used bookstores around town or, often, at a flea market near my house. The flea market was on North Lamar Boulevard, and to a pair of teenagers, it might as well have been on the Silk Road. It smelled of incense and cloves; its various nooks and crannies were filled with dusty items, from beat-up black and white TVs to sewing machines to playing cards.

It was a veritable gold mine for us because it also had a used book section, and we would spend hours there rummaging through the shelves destined for baseball treasures. One day, while perusing the sports section, we discovered a tattered and worn paperback named *Ball Four*. The book cast an irreverent look at the 1969 Seattle Pilots, an MLB expansion team made up of the players no other teams wanted. It was just like our team, Climate Engineering, full of rejects and malcontents.

Ball Four was the first "tell-all" book describing life in Major League Baseball. Jim Bouton, the author, made a fortune over the years but ruined his standing among players as the first one to go beneath the facade of the heroic major leaguer. Bouton filled the pages with snide comments as he challenged the authoritarian structure of the game when no one else would. To a couple of budding sports journalists like Selber and myself, it was our bible. Soon we were quoting phrases from it and labeling other players with the nicknames that came out of the book. None were complimentary, and it wasn't long before we were the general nemesis of our coaching staff and the scourge of the dugout.

Even though we were two of the better players, I sensed that our teammates only tolerated us and didn't respect us as team captains. The coaches even pulled us aside one day and tried to reason with us to be better role models but, being thirteen, we felt it was our duty to stand up to authority and buck the system. In reality, we were just a couple of jackasses, which showed as our team finished next to last. I look back on that summer with regret, knowing that in that slim moment, I wasted an opportunity to be more of a leader, a lesson learned the hard way.

Selber and I were such non-conformists that we saved up our allowances, bought Rawlings wooden bats, and became the only players in the league to use them when everyone else used Easton aluminum. Selber, as only he could, broke his in the first game, but I hung on to mine for a few games before it succumbed to general misuse and being sawed off by overpowering pitching. Still, I hit over .300 and envisioned myself once again as a member of the All-Star team. But, just as when I was eleven, my name was not called. Instead, Selber and I wound up by ourselves, hitting grounders and fly balls to each other for the rest of the hot, sticky afternoons.

I have no doubt my coach didn't even nominate me due to how I behaved, so I became consumed with returning the following year stronger and better than before, and with a little less attitude. The next season I made the All-Stars. Selber did not, for which he never forgave me. He continues to this day to claim he outhit me, and I made it only because I was a "name player," a term he had cobbled from *Ball Four*.

When I turned fifteen, I was ready for the COLT League, trying to fit baseball in among bagging groceries and other jobs to earn money so I could drive myself to the games with my hardship driver's license. I finally left my position as catcher and moved to second base, where a player of my smallish size could be more effective. I hadn't faced Dunnigan in more than a year since he was one year older and had been in the COLT League for a season. But as in PONY League, when I faced him twice, he was, again, simply unhittable. I never came close to anything resembling solid contact off him.

But then, strangely, fortune seemed to turn for me. And it came at the expense of Dunnigan. Somewhere along the way, he hurt his arm and couldn't play the final part of the season or in the All-Star tournaments. That meant someone, an alternate, would have to take his spot on the All-Star team, and that alternate, ironically, was me. Dunnigan's arm injury became my golden opportunity as this team was loaded. I knew we would go far, and I couldn't have been more elated to make the team, even if by the skin of my teeth.

Our first obstacle, though, was Delwood. They were again a powerhouse, loaded with tons of talent. Besides us, there was no better league in the city and, most likely, the entire state. We knew if we wanted to make it to the regional tournament in Oklahoma and, ultimately, the COLT League World Series, we would have to go through them. Delwood had come off a year where they had gone to the same regional tournament we were gunning for and played a team from Hollywood, Florida, for the right to go to the World Series. They were leading the championship game in the last inning when their shortstop dropped a popup and let the winning run score.

Mark Sheeran, who later became my best adult friend, was on that team and told me how everyone cried at the trophy presentation. He said he threw his second-place trophy into the ground as they knew they had the better team and should've gone to the World Series in Lafayette, Indiana. So here they were, back one year later, and Sheeran, nicknamed Spark, was now a starter for them. I envied how they walked onto the field, measured and aware, knowing they expected to return to Oklahoma to get what was rightfully theirs.

We played on one of the sultry Austin evenings that summer when the sun seemingly never went down, and the mosquitoes hovered, always nearby. All our friends and parents and many other baseball types from around Austin were in the stands at the YMCA fields along Town Lake, and soon the game grew into what we thought it would be, nip and tuck with neither side giving much. In the last inning, we were desperately trying to hold on to a lead when Delwood loaded the bases with Spark on second. Someone got a hit, and he came around to score the tying run.

But soon, a commotion broke out at the plate amidst animated shouting and finger-pointing. Spark protested vigorously to the umpire while both teams gathered to see what was causing the stir. After a few minutes of back and forth, the ump finally cut through the din and signaled that Spark was out. He had missed home plate! The game was over! UHO had beaten Delwood, and *we* were headed to Oklahoma for the regional tournament! They had suffered another devastating defeat, and instead, it would be our turn to go up against teams from all over the country.

I still remember arriving in Lawton, Oklahoma, for the regional tournament. It was a double-elimination affair at Cameron University's home, a more prominent and manicured field than anything we had ever played on. But we were at home in that ring, with well-deserved confidence. In sports, self-assurance is mercurial, a trait that can reveal itself in different ways. I often watched the other teams warm up before the game and listened to their chatter, each group having slightly different mannerisms and personalities. Some used standard baseball jargon, while others had more colloquial banter. The accents differed from ours and how they wore their uniform seemed slightly askew. It set in motion something I always did whenever I played an unfamiliar team. I watched them get loose, discerning how they interacted and carried themselves. I could usually figure out if we could beat them by that alone.

On the schedule we saw a team from Florida again, not Hollywood, but Hialeah, another suburb outside of Miami. We stayed in a local college dormitory and ate with our parents, which usually meant our mothers. They ensured our uniforms were washed, and we hadn't forgotten our gloves or cleats. We were fifteen and sixteen years old, seemingly men, but really just boys.

Hialeah, on the other hand, were *already* men. Those guys looked as if they could've already been parents themselves. They were Cuban, and all of them seemed to be twenty-three or twenty-four years old when they were supposed to be our age. They had beards and wore gold chains; we could hear them coming in from the bars late at night, singing and drunk. It was like we were drawing stick figures while they were sculpting in clay. They had a pitcher being scouted by the Reds, and he was the first honest-to-goodness guy any of us had seen who could hit 90 mph.

Sure enough, we drew them in the first game, and it was a rout. Neither of us had ever lost a game, but they had not only never lost, no one had ever scored on them. And that streak held up. The score was 10–0 by the time I even got into the game. It was the final inning, and the 90-mph guy was still pitching. I had seen nothing like him before. Not even Dunnigan could throw that hard. He had perfect mechanics. I couldn't even see the ball once it left his hand. Yet, amazingly, he walked me, and eventually I worked my way around to third. Our next hitter popped up into short right field for an easy out. I tagged up and went halfway down the line but turned back when I saw the throw coming in. The ball sailed wide, pulling the catcher away from the plate, and there is no question I would've scored. The third baseman looked at me and said, in his Cuban accent, "Ju would haf made eet."

Everyone on our team was mad and screaming at me. It would've been the first run scored ever given up by this team and perhaps given us some confidence heading into the rest of the tournament, and I knew it was a blunder. It was my rare chance to contribute, and I had blown it. No excuses. My teammates could barely look at me when the game was over. I remember one player, though, Terry Neitsch, a great all-around athlete and one of the best players on our team. He reached out his hand and said, "Shake it off, Squid. Your run wouldn't have made any difference." I always respected him for that because it made me feel included, knowing we won together and lost together as a unit.

Still, it was little consolation as this was the first time we had ever lost a game, and some players were looking to place blame. And since I had blown it so severely, naturally, I was the goat. But it was 10–0, and after about twenty minutes, everyone realized that we had simply been outclassed. My mistake was no different from all the other ones we made in that game. I learned you must take advantage of your opportunities when they present themselves, regardless of the potential outcome. It probably explains why I decided to play again so many years later.

We clawed our way back through the losers bracket, playing teams from Georgia and Tennessee, and watched Hialeah plow through everyone and knew they were destined for the championship game. They were actually fun to watch. The players and the fans did many team cheers throughout the game, and soon I became infected with their spirit. Since I hadn't had much playing time, I figured I might contribute to our fortunes by mimicking one of their cheers, elevating us to their level. During one game, I got into the spirit and jumped out in front of our fans and exhorted:

"Arriba, Arriba, Sis boom bah,

UHO, UHO, rah rah rah!"

All the parents joined in, and the players got a big kick out of it. I was finally out of the doghouse, my mistake from the earlier game forgotten.

Sure enough, we made it back to the finals and in front of us was none other than Hialeah. This time, we managed to eke out the first runs they had ever given up. We led much of the game, although a sense of foreboding permeated the small collegiate park. We led by a run with two outs in the last inning, but they loaded the bases. Our pitcher tried to pick the runner off first but threw it away, and the tying and winning runs came around to score. And suddenly, we were Delwood all over again. We were the Austin team that had blown the game in the last inning, letting a Florida team go to the World Series. Two years in a row!

Instead of heading to the COLT League World Series in Indiana, we drove straight through the night back to Texas. I rode with one of my teammate's parents, trying to ease the sting of defeat by edging closer and closer to their daughter in the back seat. Although she barely even knew I was there, it didn't matter. Her presence gave me something to ponder besides the sound of rubber on the asphalt and the most thrilling baseball season I had ever experienced.

It was a devastating loss and something that still bothers me today when I recall how good that team was. I think about that summer often and realize how lucky I was to have even been among that great group of athletes. I knew, and everyone else did too, that had Dunnigan been able to play, we were probably the best team in the country. But had Dunnigan played, I wouldn't have been there. I knew my role was not to be the star or even a player given much responsibility, but it was important to be a part of something bigger than myself. I realized how every piece mattered. Maybe had I scored in that first game, that one run might have been enough for us to believe in ourselves and hold on to the lead the next round. You never know, maybe my role was simply to lead them in a cheer.

Sometimes it is hard to understand the impact of something while you are experiencing it. It takes reflection and context to recognize its value. I know I began on that team unsure of how to fit in, and even though there were slipups, I had grown as a ball-player and as a person. I took what arguably could be considered a moment of weakness and turned it into a strength, something I only grasped later in life. When we got back to town, I was asked by the coaching staff, the only one out of all the players, if I would give a speech at the team banquet a few weeks later. It was an honor, and a moment I still cherish today.

I had every reason to believe that next year would be more of the same, but it wasn't. My sixteen-year-old team simply dominated the entire league during the regular season. I don't think we lost a game, and I hit .715. But in the All-Stars, we never made it out of the first tournament. Somehow we lost two games in the first round, and that was it. My summers would no longer be filled with games where little brothers played "cup ball" behind the backstop, and foul balls were returned to the concession stands for a Coke. Instead, it was time to move on to the high school game, where men were paid to coach and scouts sat in the stands instead of mothers. The following years would allow me to see how far I could take my "career." I didn't realize it then, but I was much closer to the end than I thought.

CHAPTER 6

IS THIS HEAVEN?

I'd walk through hell in a gasoline suit to play baseball.

—Pete Rose

Back at Downs Field, I momentarily stepped out of the box and looked out at the mound until my eyes met Dunnigan's. Once he realized it was me at the plate, a smile spread across his face, and he yelled out, "Squiiiidd!"

I couldn't help but grin back, and all the tension melted away, two old friends seeing each other for the first time in decades. He looked the same in 2022 as he did nearly forty years ago, handsome and broad-shouldered. And as I discovered later, he was married with an athletic family and had spent most of his adult life in insurance. The arm problems he had when we were younger effectively ended his hopes of a professional career. It was great to see him again, but the first pitch he sailed my way came up under my chin as he tried to get an advantage, and I flew back, almost falling over.

It was still the same old Joe, but it wasn't the same old me. It was harder to pick up the ball from his hand, and it seemed like I would lose track of it as it neared the plate. I only had a couple of outings of batting practice when the pitches were moving at the same speed, with no one throwing any curves. However, facing someone trying to get you out was a different matter. So, when the 3–1 pitch drifted mercifully outside, I was overcome with relief and could begin a slow trot to first base. I was in a baseball game for the first time in thirty years and somehow got on base. And against Joe Dunnigan, of all people.

For a moment it seemed like a dream, but I knew it was real because the next batter hit a ground ball, and I had to run with everything I had to make it to second. I eventually worked my way to third base, and soon there was a passed ball, which meant I had to race for the plate. In my mind, I ran effortlessly and with great swiftness, beating the throw by a mile. But after watching a video Elliott shot, it was evident I labored to initiate a simple running motion. My gait had a noticeable limp, such that the catcher went to the backstop and retrieved the ball with enough time to toss it to Dunnigan, with me having just crossed the plate by the time it arrived. I scored standing up, although sliding never entered my mind. It became clear when I got home, though, I was walking with a pronounced limp, and I knew that my burgeoning baseball career would not come without a price.

I also knew that baseball would be much more fun if Elliott were around to enjoy it, so I once again began my quest to get in touch with the Playboys rather than continue with the over-fifty team. After digging around the internet, I eventually discovered the Playboys' website, but it seemed as if the only way to get involved would be to join their fan club, and I wasn't sure what that meant.

But providence intervened just as I was about to give up all hope. My wife met a woman who was friends with a player on the team. Liz told her about my "comeback" attempt and my desire to get in touch with them. She gave Liz the email address of a Playboy named Dave Mead. I emailed Dave and told him that a friend and I were interested in playing in the sandlot league and with the Playboys if they had room on the team. Dave was gracious enough to email me back but was honest and upfront about joining the team. He said as if from a script, they had a deep roster, and the best thing would be to watch a game at the Long Time and introduce myself around.

He copied a teammate named Howard Carey on his response, and Howard replied their next game was in mid-May, but if I was interested in taking a few cuts, he had a batting cage in East Austin, aptly named "The Meantime." It wasn't exactly what I had hoped for, but it was a start. I had broken through and made contact with someone who was now, at least, pointing me in the right direction. I filed it away in the back of my mind as I plotted to go out to the Long Time in May, armed and ready to work my way onto the Playboys. There was only one problem: I still couldn't play because my knee was aching, and I had no one to go with me. Elliott was going to be out of commission for a while due to his work schedule. He was now running an investment firm and sat on several boards, so despite being "retired" from Nike, he was by no means sitting idly by.

I thought about asking a couple of other friends to come along but deep down knew it would be too difficult to explain. Playing baseball in the fifty-and-over league wasn't advertised among my friends except for the videos Elliott had sent of our early exploits in the cage. No one knew he and I were determined to play baseball again, and no one cared that we were angling to play in something called sandlot baseball.

By the time the second weekend in May rolled around, I had summoned my courage and drove out to the Long Time by myself, ready to walk right into the action. The Long Time is in a little town called Webberville, just east of Austin. It is set a couple hundred yards off a two-lane road, and you would never see it if you didn't know where you were going. But once you turned off the main road and pulled up, it was unmistakable that you were about to experience something like never before.

There was this old sign that looked like something a cowboy on mescaline would've made, alerting everyone to the fact that you are now at "The Long Time." Just inside the gate is an old farmhouse up on blocks, and all around was a vibe of understated coolness as kids ran and played, dogs barked, and people lounged about on metal chairs. I sat in a chair against what seemed to be an old wooden office (later, I discovered this was where Jack ran his design studio). Despite the constant music played throughout the game, there was a feeling of serenity. The colors swirled around, and at first, it seemed very familiar. I heard ballplayers calling, "Come on now, rock your fire. Here we go, babe, one time, one time."

It appeared that I had gone back in time. Everything seemed to be from the turn of the twentieth century. Old-timey signs and a hand-painted scoreboard stood above a snack bar made of wood, and a dugout I'm certain housed a rooster. Someone standing on a ladder kept score by hand. The fans were dressed in what I could only describe as hipster attire. There were several ill-fitting black pants that seemed out of place at a baseball game, with weird socks and T-shirts that were too tight. Everyone in the stands wore beards and odd-shaped hats.

In the background, I could see a ballgame with players running around a field carved into a small area beside a creek. It seemed like a movie set, and when I moved closer, it was as if I had walked into the movie itself, like when the players appeared out of the corn in *Field of Dreams*. They were asking, "Is this heaven?" And just as when I watched the video for the first time, that is exactly how I felt. It was baseball heaven.

For a moment, I thought I was at a small-town weekend festival, yet I knew, having watched the video, that I was at a Texas Playboys baseball game. It was ground zero for the sandlot revolution sweeping across the county. More than a hundred teams had formed since the mid-2000s when Jack started the Playboys and gave birth to the entire crusade. While an architecture student at Auburn University, Jack had built a backstop for a sandlot team in rural Alabama who had been playing continuously for nearly eighty years. He resolved then that one day he would bring a team of his own back to play against them. Years later, he started the Playboys to do just that. His team outgrew itself and became two teams, then four. Then, teams began popping up in cities like Nashville and Tulsa and as far away as Vancouver. From the San Jose Prune Pickers on the West Coast to the Radio City Rockefellers in New York. Teams begat leagues in states like North Carolina and cities such as New Orleans, with their own brand of sandlot called the People's Baseball league. Large cities, small towns, and unknown hopefuls interspersed among big names, all living their unique history. Music star Jack White had a team. So did the clothing designer Billy Reid. And despite my earlier protestations, I knew I wanted to be part of it too.

The Playboys were playing a team from El Paso, the Diablitos. The players seemed athletic enough, and the pitcher was throwing about as hard as I had seen in my fifty-and-over league, if not harder. The teams consisted of all types, men, women, young, and old. And so, I sat watching, transfixed by the action and listening to the music, the songs playing during the action. Sometimes they stopped, and I heard the murmur of conversations in the stands. Occasionally, I heard only the umpire's calls. It was the baseball I remember from my childhood dreams, something I had always imagined could be but had never found until now.

I wanted to introduce myself to Howard. I had seen his face on Instagram, so I knew what he looked like, but after searching the field, I couldn't locate him. My heart sank, and I wondered if the entire trip would be a waste of time. But as the Playboys got the third out and ran off the field, a jolt came over me when the catcher took off his mask. There he was. Howard Carey, the only conduit I had to sandlot baseball, and he was jogging off the field and heading right toward me. It was the culmination of what had begun with a conversation with an old friend more than a year ago, and now the opportunity to turn that discussion into reality presented itself directly in front of me.

Howard went into the dugout and took off his equipment, and I waited for the right moment to say hello. Sure enough, he emerged from inside and began to talk to people nearby. I noticed the players spent as much time in the stands—talking with family and friends, holding babies, and posing for pictures—as they did in the dugout or on the field. As Howard came near me, I reached out and introduced myself, and we began to talk. He was gracious and patient and didn't seem to mind my interminable line of questioning. Even though technically in the middle of a game, he answered every question and discussed what was going on at length.

Eventually, Howard introduced me to a guy who had been sitting next to me the whole time. His name was Wes Paparone, and he was the coach of another local team called the Lovejoys. Paydirt! I had two contacts from the sandlot league, and the day wasn't even half over. Wes and I sat and talked the rest of the game, discussing what the league was about and how to become a part of it.

At the end of the game, Howard brought over a couple of his teammates and introduced them, and in short order, I felt like I was part of the family even though I had done nothing more than come out to watch them play. Howard said I should come by his batting cage sometime, so I agreed. I told him I would bring a friend with me, and we'd drop by The Meantime and take a few cuts.

I called Elliott immediately and reported to him what had happened. In two short hours, I went from a guy who barely knew how to find the place to knowing two coaches and having all the ins and outs of being a part of the league. The goal was still to get on the Playboys, and I told Elliott I had found the right guy. Howard was one of the original members and had some status within the construct of the team. I said we were invited for batting practice at his cage, apparently in the back of his house. After a second of what I am certain was bewildered reflection, we agreed to meet at Howard's later in the week to try to move a step closer to our goal of playing sandlot baseball on the Playboys.

A few days later, I met Elliott at Howard's place. He lived in a neighborhood on the east side of town. It stood in what had once been one of the worst parts of the city, the other side of the tracks. A former haven of drug deals, violence, and generally whatever mayhem Austin could work itself into, it wasn't far from where Elliott and I grew up in the 1970s and '80s. But lately, as with most cities that changed at the turn of this century, the neighborhood was reborn. Several new restaurants and nightspots filled the main streets while new residents built homes on every corner. It was the locus of the hipster movement turning the town from a state government sloth into a high-tech cheetah. The streets were cleaner, the colors brighter, and everything moved faster.

There were still signs of the area's former coating of trash with assorted cars on blocks, but at the forefront was a transcendence propelling the city into a new era. And as much as Elliott and I were relics seemingly from the previous incarnation of the town, we were also firsthand participants in the new, leading edge of Austin's transformative identity. Sandlot baseball was part of this identity, and we were on the cusp of being a part of it. We just had to talk our way in.

Howard's house was on an oversized lot; behind it, a shed. Inside, I later learned, was where sandlot teams of not only the Playboys but all the other teams and players of this burgeoning league gathered at various times to hit. Howard had fashioned a net with a pitching machine and decorated the facility's walls with old posters and other classic baseball memorabilia. It was a baseball haven, and upon entering, Elliott and I shared a couple of knowing glances at each other. Unlike the first team we encountered, this place made more sense. It seemed so far away from the batting cage where we had been only a few weeks before, where the players looked desperately uninspired by our arrival.

SHINE THE LIGHT

As opposed to the reception we had received before, Howard was warm and inviting and explained in great detail about the league, his team, and how, quite honestly, there was simply no room for us on it.

CHAPTER 7

GET IN THERE

Baseball is like driving, it's the one who gets home safely that counts.

—Tommy Lasorda

The return to Austin from the near miss at the COLT League tournament in Oklahoma coincided with the beginning of the new school year. Spark pounced upon me as I strolled into the open-air atrium of our high school, Reagan, and looked for my locker. I hadn't seen him since he missed home plate earlier in the summer, his dab of shame resulting in my team's smidge of glory. Upon seeing my regional tournament T-shirt he immediately asked what had happened.

This was long before cell phones and the internet. At that time, we weren't necessarily communicating by chiseling letters into a granite slab. Still, if you wanted to find out about something, you had to wait until the opportunity presented itself. Spark had little idea what had happened to my team since we walked off the field after our game in Austin and had been waiting for the rest of the summer to hear from me.

I shared the Hialeah saga of how we lost to an all-star team from Florida in the final inning, with a chance to go to the World Series. The story was so pitiful that it was only natural for him to reach out and give me a big hug. We had become good friends through our mutual interest in sports, particularly baseball. He and his Irish band of brothers had moved to Austin in the 1970s. They were from California and were typical of that era's freewheeling West Coast lifestyle—full of character, alternately fighting and carousing but more important, they were athletic and intelligent. Often during high school, we sat up late at night on the phone, talking about girls and sports but usually about baseball.

Spark lived in a different neighborhood when we were in elementary school but raced home after classes let out to watch the same MLB playoff games on TV as I did, except he was a Pirates fan while I was pulling for the Reds. Growing up, we had read many of the same books, like the John R. Tunis series featuring the character Highpockets and, like Selber, the other standout baseball tomes from legends like Roger Angell and Roger Kahn.

He genuinely felt sorry for what my team had gone through, as he was in the unique position to know the same feeling. And he knew that he was partly responsible for us even getting that far after missing home plate in the championship game against us. But, we knew, despite the sadness of youth baseball ending in such dramatic fashion for both of us, the bigger fish of high school baseball was what lay ahead. Besides, I needed a new confidant as Selber wound up going to a rival school, and with all the unique issues and drama that high school brings, his presence in my life moved to the back burner.

Entering high school in 1979, I was a thirteen-year-old punk with braces to accompany my mustache. I was also a full year younger than everyone else. While in the second grade, my parents did what they thought was the smart thing and had me skip from the first grade to the third. Unfortunately, it was the exact opposite thing to do for someone interested in playing competitive sports as a teenager, especially when one year of growth and maturity can make such an enormous difference in a developing body.

Additionally, the complex emotional roller coaster that is entry into high school, and navigating the societal norms and customs of a decidedly older student body, was complex. Hairstyles seemed to ensure social status then, particularly for people who parted theirs in the middle and had wings to either side. Unfortunately, my hair didn't part down the middle, and wings were out of the question. I was beset with braces, a 100-pound body, and a big mouth, a decidedly poor mix. Still, I made the freshman basketball team, and high school sports seemed like an extension of Little League until I realized this team would be unlike any I had been on before.

In the late seventies and early eighties, Reagan High School's student population featured an assortment of races, ethnicities, and cultural backgrounds. The school was split 55 percent white and 45 percent minority. Being a mixture of two different nationalities, Mexican and American, I moved easily through most worlds. But when I made the freshman team, it was the first time I would undoubtedly be in the minority. I was the only white person on an otherwise all-Black squad; they called me "Spot." It was hilarious but not unexpected. Growing up in Northeast Austin, I had several close African American friends. Many elementary and junior high classmates were Black, and everyone in our neighborhood played together, regardless of race or ethnicity. This wasn't always the case, however. It had been a tumultuous decade for race relations in the area. Reagan had experienced race riots in the early seventies along with another nearby school. But by the time we enrolled in the latter part of the decade, tensions had cooled, and despite the typical confrontations that inevitably accompany kids in their adolescent years, most of the people at our school got along just fine.

As for the basketball team, one player, in particular, stood out from the rest of us. He would eventually become one of my best friends at Reagan and someone I still hold in tremendous regard. His name was Gerald Wright, and he was the single person who made me understand that I would not become a professional baseball player. He was the best player on our freshman team and also played on the varsity, where he was one of the better players. As one of the school's best natural athletes, he was as good in baseball as basketball. He would've been the quarterback on the football team if he had chosen to play that sport. As it was, we were allowed to try out for baseball later than everyone else since we were on the basketball team.

There was a clear distinction between Gerald and me when we showed up as the only two players left to evaluate. He was not only better than me, but it didn't help when he, not knowing any better, grabbed a fungo bat during BP and drilled shots into the gap. A wrist injury in one of our final team practices kept me from holding the bat, but I couldn't let the coach know I was hurt and would need another ten days to adequately compete. They would be well into their season by then. And after cobbling a few weak grounders to shortstop, the coach told me with a certain clarity that perhaps I should try again next year. And just as when I was eleven and thirteen and did not make the All-Star teams, I was once again on the outside looking in. I watched all my pals playing on the JV and knew I would need to devote myself to the game during the offseason to become stronger and better.

So back to the drawing board I went in the offseason. As a sophomore, I first let the basketball coach know I would *not* be going out for the JV. He didn't seem too disappointed, and I knew there was no future for me there. Instead, I asked around to see who wanted to practice baseball and found a group of older players, guys starting on the varsity, and discovered they worked out every day after school at a nearby field. These players were much bigger and more talented than me and would work out no matter how cold it was. Working with them gave me the agency necessary to create my own future. My arm strengthened, my batting eye sharpened, and by the time tryouts rolled around again in the spring, I not only made the JV but by a couple of weeks into the season, they called me up to the varsity for an out-of-town weekend trip. The coach gave me the smallest varsity uniform, which draped around my skinny body so sloppily they called me "Trash Bag." I didn't care, though. I went from being cut as a freshman to making the varsity as a sophomore, even if just for a day.

The JV season went along pretty uneventfully. I started at second base and led off, knowing the offseason workouts with the older players had prepared me to achieve. Until once again it came to a crashing end. We were playing at Anderson High in what was then the tony Northwest Hills, where all the rich kids lived, when I got hit with a pitch on the tip of my fingers. It didn't hurt, but the tips of the pinky and ring finger on my right hand were bloody and swollen. Back then, there was no first aid kit, so I wrapped my hand in a towel and waited until the game was over. When I got home, my parents didn't seem to think it was a big deal, but we got X-rays. Sure enough, I had suffered two broken bones right on the ends of my fingers. I was out for the year and with it, another season lost. Except this time, fortune smiled down upon me. The JV season ended before the varsity, and the coach knew I had been having a good year, so he invited me to rejoin them once my fingers healed. A few weeks later, I was back on the varsity, this time for good.

I didn't see any action until the season's final game, and then only by accident. It was the last inning, and we had a slow runner on first base. The coach tried to find someone to step in and run. He looked at Spark, who was now a junior and playing backup center field. He said, "Sheeran, get in there!" Spark turned to the coach, "Coach, I forgot my cleats." I quickly looked down and realized he was wearing Converse All Stars instead of regular cleats. At this point, the coach, disgusted, looked at another player, Buddy Hughes, and roared, "Hughes, get in there!!" Hughes instantly declared, "Coach, I brought the wrong jersey."

Pat Pennington was our head baseball coach. Hired to coach the perennial state playoff football program, his wrangling of us on the baseball field in the spring was merely an afterthought. It was a job in name only, as he would usually cut our practices short and head to where the football team was conducting spring workouts, leaving us to finish by ourselves. He only wanted to coach football and didn't want to waste his time with misfits like us (as anyone can see why). So, apparently out of options, he looked up and down the bench, rubbing his hand along his chin before he spied me sitting down at the end, trying to avoid any controversy.

"Matthews, get in there . . . I guess," he said less than enthusiastically.

I wanted to play it cool, but inside I was ecstatic. This was my chance to finally feel like I was a varsity baseball player at Reagan High School. The school of my dreams and the moment of my ascendency into the annals of big-time baseball. This was my moment; it was my time!

I promptly got picked off before the pitcher even threw a pitch, but miraculously, the ump missed the call, and I was safe back at the bag. Coach Pennington hadn't noticed what only myself and the first baseman had, that I was out by a foot. Somehow escaping all calamity, I lived to see another day. This time I stepped off the base as carefully as a guy trying to walk a tightrope, taking about two baby steps off first and didn't stray far from there. My heart was beating so fast I could barely catch my breath. Soon enough, someone hit a ground ball, and they made the play, and mercifully the inning and the season were over. Attention to detail became a mantra from that moment forward. It was essential to be ready at all times and for anything, including the pitcher throwing over to first base in a meaningless contest.

By the time my junior year trundled around, I was a surefire player and started the season at second base. Our team was pretty stacked, but there were several great players around town, including Joe Dunnigan, who was pitching at a rival school (coincidentally with Selber). He was by now one of the top pitchers in the state, much less our district. And it was against Dunnigan that I would suffer one of the most humbling moments of my baseball life. It happened during a Friday night game with an unusually large crowd of fans in the stands at Nelson Field, where we typically played our home games.

Nelson Field was a fabulous high school baseball park deep-set behind the football stadium and a place I loved to play. It was where I felt most comfortable until late in the game, with the bases loaded and Dunnigan on the hill. He threw a fastball past me and then grinned slightly as he mixed in a curve that left me flat-footed to take the count to 0–2. I knew he would come back with the heater, and I was ready to time it up and swing, but instead, the same silly grin came across his face (I can still see it in my sleep over forty years later), and he floated a soft curve that buckled me at the knees. I struck out with the bases loaded and not once lifted the bat off my shoulder.

Coach Pennington yelled, "Hughes, get in at second base!!" (I guess he brought the correct jersey this time.) But he didn't need to say anything. I knew I was benched. I heard him tell our scorekeeper, "Put a star next to that. No, put two stars!" It was the first time a coach had told me to get off the field, and not even the sunken dugouts of Nelson Field could provide enough shelter from his cold, icy glare that was lasered on me for the rest of the game. I ended up slinking out and riding home in silence. I wasn't sure what would happen at practice the next day, but I knew it wouldn't be good.

At the next day's practice, I found another player standing in front of me at second base. My stint as the starter was over. I was assured of never stepping on the field for the rest of the season. But, as luck would have it, one starter got into an argument with the coach and abruptly quit the team, causing a shift in the positions. I was quickly inserted back into the starting lineup. I still remember Coach coming toward me before practice that day, "Matthews, you are back in, hitting second. Practice your bunting." I got the message. In no uncertain terms, he was telling me I had talent but had to be more assertive. I had to be willing to create my own luck and go after things if I was going to make a difference. I had to understand it wasn't Little League, where everyone clapped for you for giving your best effort. For the coach, it was his livelihood. For the players, it was to honor the ones before and create a legacy for those who came after. It was also the last time I would not start in a high school baseball game.

Junior year turned into my senior year, and I made the All-District and All-Centex teams, and being known around town as a good player was about all I could ask. I knew I wasn't going to be a pro, though. I was sure I wasn't even going to be a college player, not after watching Gerald play such a beautiful form of shortstop right next to me. Watching him gobble up grounders, making throws from all angles, and hitting the ball into the gap time after time, I knew how a real player looked. The Braves drafted him at the end of our senior year, and he wound up taking batting practice with the team in Fulton County Stadium in Atlanta. He never signed, however, choosing instead to play college basketball at New Mexico State.

But, now, stripped of ego, came an acknowledgment of life's larger picture and the search to find my place in it. So, when my coach asked me if I wanted to continue playing in college, I told him no. He knew other coaches at places like Ranger Junior College and San Jacinto (both of which were excellent baseball schools and perfect feeder programs into Division I programs across the state). But I had a full academic scholarship to the University of Texas, and I knew that baseball had become more of a goal-minded pursuit rather than an employment opportunity. Yet, I wasn't content to sit back, enjoy the summer, and prepare for my first year of college.

SHINE THE LIGHT

I had spent countless days and nights making something out of myself through baseball, enduring interminable missteps and pratfalls. Why stop now? All the lessons I had been taught, all the blunders I had made, all the time spent practicing when no one else was. There had to be a payoff somewhere. Why not try to walk on at UT? How hard could it be? I was All-District. I was All-Centex. And with the certainty that comes only with youth I marched to campus one day in late August and patrolled through the athletic offices until I discovered a door that read CLIFF GUSTAFSON, HEAD BASEBALL COACH.

I shuffled my feet in front of Coach Gus's door, working up the nerve to knock. Suddenly, my knees went weak when I realized what I was doing. His Longhorn team had just won college baseball's national championship with players such as Roger Clemens, Calvin Schiraldi, and Spike Owen. Those three formed the nucleus of the Boston Red Sox three years later in one of the greatest baseball games of all time, the sixth game of the 1986 World Series.

I had prepared a great speech about how good I was and what I could offer, but after hearing his voice from behind the door calling me in, all I could muster was, "Coach Gus, I would like to try out for the team this year." He never looked up at me from the newspaper he was reading but murmured something like, "Okay, be out at the field on Monday at three thirty," and turned the page. I told him thank you and ran out of there like a child with a stolen cookie. He had probably already mentally cut me just by watching my knees shake. But on my first day of college, I loaded up my glove and cleats and headed to Disch-Falk Field, parked my car and wandered down to the field with thirty other guys, all of whom stood around while the reigning national champions practiced. Very few of us, it seemed, had a shot.

Disch-Falk Field was a place I had been coming to since I was a kid. Built in the 1970s, it was a signature example of the wealth and affluence of the University of Texas, which sat on billions of dollars of oil fields in the western part of the state. A clam shell roof covered most of the nearly seven thousand seats, as opposed to extended backstops, which were the norm for most college programs of that era. It was the goal of every baseball kid to play there someday. I spent many spring afternoons watching doubleheaders of the great Longhorn teams in the late seventies and early eighties. During spring break, Texas used to play a doubleheader every day against schools from all over the country. While all the other kids were at the beach, I was at Disch-Falk, studying baseball and idolizing all the players on the field, hoping to emulate them one day.

Schiraldi, an All-American and a legendary high school pitcher in the area, was a friend of my family. Our parents used to play bridge together on the occasional weekend. But my favorite player was Spike Owen. He was an All-American shortstop and my idol. (Ironically enough, Coby Kerlin, one of my friends from the previously mentioned UHO All-Star team, would also become an All-American shortstop at Texas.)

One time, Selber and I were hanging outside the locker room after a game, hoping to meet some players, when Spike came striding up the stairs toward us. We stopped him and asked for an autograph. At that point, Selber said, "Good game, Spike." He nodded and said thank you while signing the paper in front of him. He then looked over at me, whereupon I looked straight into his eyes and shouted in his general direction for some unknown reason, "Thank you." For a moment, he looked puzzled, then signed my scorecard and handed it back to me. I immediately turned around and walked away, forever shamed.

Once the varsity team finished practicing, the walk-ons paired up and threw. One guy walked up and asked if I wanted to throw, and I said sure, so we tossed the ball together. For the next three weeks, he was my warm-up partner and general sounding board for all things on how to make the team. His name was Brian Cisarik, and he made the team and became a two-time all-conference outfielder. He still holds the school record for the highest single-season batting average at .429. I felt he would do well when ringing doubles off the wall at the Disch, which is no small feat. It's a vast yard, and when you hit the wall on the fly three or four times in a row during batting practice, it gets people's attention, especially legendary coaches.

I had a decent enough showing on the field and at the plate to have some confidence, so when the three weeks were up, it was time for Coach Gus to let us know who had made it. I felt good about my chances, so it was no surprise when he came out of the stands and told us to gather around, and made a beeline right for me. No doubt he remembered my sterling performance in his office and my stellar play on the field. He stopped next to me, put his arm around my shoulder, and said, "If I call your name, you need to report for practice with the regular team on Monday." It was like we were best friends. I knew at that point I had made the team and imagined how proud my friends and family would be when I informed them how I had walked on to play for the defending College World Series Champions, the University of Texas Longhorns!

(Coach Gus passed away, sadly, at the age of ninety-one, just prior to the publishing of this book. His legacy on college baseball is unmatched.)

CHAPTER 8
WHISKEY AND LEATHER

One of the greatest things about baseball is that you do not need much to play. All you need is a bat and a ball—not even a glove—and a whole lot of imagination.

—David Ortiz

"We have too many guys," Howard said, almost before we had even asked. The dream of getting on the Playboys was over. "We have nearly sixty players on our roster; everybody is always complaining about not getting enough playing time. So, it's really difficult to add new guys to the team." He paused and added, "But you know what you should do . . . " His voice trailed off.

I liked Howard from the moment I met him. He was from Kentucky, and I could see from the baseball memorabilia spread throughout the batting cage that we were cut from the same cloth, both of us fans of Cincinnati's Big Red Machine. Elliott and I had gone to the cage not only to take some batting practice but also to feel him out for how we could get onto the Playboys. It was clear Howard got requests all the time from the wannabes and hangers-on, so he was polite but wary of us from the beginning. He told us how Jack had grown the team from a small group of local ballplayers and friends fifteen years ago into what it is now, a roster with nearly sixty players from all over the state.

Back then, they would repeatedly play against each other in an open park in town. But that team grew, and soon there was another team. And then there were a couple more, and before you knew it, Austin had a bona fide league of sandlot teams. The number was up to eleven now and growing by the day. But the Playboys, well, they had a full roster.

"You know what you should do," he started again. "You should start your own team." It was all very matter-of-fact as if he prepared this response for dozens of inquiries. For him, it seemed like something just anyone could do. "We have people hitting us up all the time to be on the Playboys. You would be the last guys on the roster and probably hardly ever play. It's just not worth it. Start your own team, and you can call your own shots, and play as much as you want. I'll even help you."

What help he could give us was anyone's guess at that time because Elliott and I stood there dumbfounded. For the moment, it seemed like having exhausted one option with the over-fifty team, we would again be on the outside looking in. Not only had we not played baseball in nearly three decades, but we knew nothing about putting a team together and nothing about how to do it in this league.

"That sounds great," Elliott chimed in, breaking the silence. I looked over at him and saw he had a slight grin on his face. And for a moment, it finally hit me. Elliott was more than just a kid I had grown up with who wanted to play baseball again. He was a savvy executive and someone who had achieved at the highest levels of international business. And I don't know why, but I guess since I know him so well, I had forgotten about who he was and what he was capable of.

Elliott had grown up the son of a single mother. His parents divorced when he was little, and he rarely spoke about his father to any of us. But his mother, Jo, was a constant presence in our lives. She was a math teacher at our high school and at whose house kids gathered following football games and other weekend nights when Elliott and his sister Julia were in school. They lived down the street from me, and I remember playing football together in the street or a neighbor's yard and seeing him around our school when we were young. He always seemed much older than me, although we were only a grade apart. We hung around most of the same people, but even at an early age, he seemed driven beyond the rest of us, as if his goals were farther away and harder to reach. When it was time to go to college, he moved away from Austin and attended TCU in Fort Worth. He had been an athletic trainer at Reagan and headed for a degree in kinesiology and, presumably, a career in sports medicine. In fact, after graduation, he became a trainer for the Dallas Cowboys, and we cheered every time we saw him on the sidelines when watching the games on TV. But medicine wasn't in his heart, and soon he was back in school at Ohio University, where he earned a master's degree in sports management.

He started at Nike right after that as an entry-level salesman. I can still picture him driving around in his minivan, which he used to make sales calls across the state. But it wasn't his natural affinity for sales that made him successful. He made it by grinding, day after day and night after night. Every time we called him, he was working. Every time we asked him how he was, he was tired. Every time we went to bed at night, he was getting on a plane and heading somewhere across the world. And after endless hours away from his family and friends, he rose in the company and soon ran all of Nike in Europe. Eventually, he and his family moved back to the US, and by the end of his career, he was running the entire company worldwide. He never let his humble beginnings stand in the way of what he wanted, and today his new goal was to start a baseball team.

"That's exactly what we'll do," he said. He looked over at me, and instantly I nodded, knowing full well that I had no idea where he was going with it, but if he was steering the ship, we were going to get there. "If you help us, Howard, we'll start our own team and come back and kick y'all's asses."

Howard laughed at that. He knew he had roped us into the sandlot baseball league on better terms than initially envisioned, and soon all three of us were huddled together, making plans for what was to become our very own team. "Just tell us what to do, and we'll get it done," Elliott implored. His eyes had glazed over by now, and I could see the wheels spinning.

"The first thing you have to do before anything else is cast your team," Howard said.

"Cast?"

"Yeah, cast . . . like a movie. Get guys who can fill a role. You want funny guys, guys who are good and some who aren't so good. You want characters. You need people to fill a specific role on the team, so it will be fun for you and entertaining for the fans." Howard's instructions seemed simple enough, and I was encouraged by what I heard. It seemed like just a matter of who we needed to get. For me, though, that was the major roadblock. I wasn't sure if I knew anyone that fit the bill. What sort of characters would we need to make it entertaining, not only for us but, as Howard said, for the fans?

Later that day, Elliott called me and told me he had ridden his bike from Howard's to his house off of South Congress with his bat sticking out of his backpack. He said he was giddy, like a school kid, and had it all figured out. And knowing him, I was confident he had. So, we agreed to meet the next day for coffee, and when we did, he hatched his plan. But before revealing the details, he told me his thoughts on owning a minor league baseball team after he retired. He had imagined himself riding a lawn mower, cutting the outfield grass, and designing things like the uniforms and all the trappings of what it would entail to run a baseball organization. He said this had been his dream, and it was right in front of us. Even beyond the baseball aspect, he said it was about creating a community where people of all types could gather without judgment and feel free to invest in something beyond themselves. So it was decided we would create a baseball team and form it in our image, the image of who we once were growing up and who we were now as adults. It would reflect the environment we grew up in and the one where we currently live. It would be an Austin original, cast down to the last detail. It was golden . . . the only problem was Elliott was going out of the country for the summer, and neither of us knew who we might "cast," so we agreed to meet when he returned in July and discuss it then.

Meanwhile, I was still trying to make a go of it with the men's league team. My knee was hurting so much, though, I could barely run. Trying to labor through a couple of warm-up sprints before the game would send excruciating pains like rays of fire through my leg. But I kept quiet and tried to stay in the outfield as much as possible. I wasn't going to quit. Not yet, anyway. And it was during one of these stints in the outfield field when it finally dawned on me. I had become the kid who would spend all of his time praying the ball wouldn't come his way, hoping to avoid the ignominy that comes with athletic failure. And sure enough, that was what I was doing when a fly ball suddenly appeared in the sky and was heading directly for me.

It was the first fly I had seen since the early nineties, and I circled under it with tiny steps like a crab crossing a beach. As the ball was coming down, I threw up my hand, and it hit my glove right in the pocket. I had it! I had made the catch! At least for a second, until I realized the ball had not only hit the pocket but gone right through it and was now rolling around on the ground. I looked up and saw the astonished hitter running again. He must've stopped thinking the ball had been caught. I could also hear the unmistakable cries of my teammates to "Get it in . . . throw it in!" I hobbled over to the ball and tossed it back to the second baseman as the runner slid into third. I couldn't even process what had taken place. I was under it, in position. The ball was in the pocket. What had happened? And then I looked at my glove. It had disintegrated upon impact, like the opening sequence of *The Six Million Dollar Man*. My glove had simply blown apart when the ball hit it. And it was at that point I realized the mitt was almost forty years old. I calculated that had I used something like that in high school, it would've been equivalent to playing with a glove from the 1940s. It was just sad.

When I got home, I realized that my Mizuno, or what was left of it, was the only glove I had, so it would be up to me to find a replacement. I remembered that my sons must've had gloves they used when they were young, so I went rummaging around in my attic trying to locate one, but there wasn't anything to be found. I was left with no option but to buy a new one, and now my return to baseball was not only humbling on the field but expensive off of it too. I had already shelled out for a bat, helmet, cleats, pants, and batting gloves, so what was the difference in adding a fielding glove to the mix? I decided to go to the sporting goods store to get a new one, but it was too late, so I made plans to go the following day.

Since I hadn't bought a glove in nearly half a century, I wasn't sure what model to get, so I decided to examine a few online. After checking out the choices on Amazon, I found myself poking around the Wilson Sporting Goods website looking at gloves called the Wilson A2000. The A2000 was the gold standard among top-quality gloves, and I always coveted owning one, but my family could never afford it. They were expensive and were only suited to higher-level players, but this would most likely be the last glove I ever bought, so why not splurge and get one? It would make me feel better about my dismal play on the field, and who knows, I might give it to one of my sons when my playing days were truly over.

For years, I had believed there was only one A2000 model, but after a few minutes on the website, I realized there were dozens in all sizes and configurations, which became the source of my growing cloudy judgment. After about twenty minutes, I finally settled on a smaller infielder's model that might, if nothing else, make me look like I belonged on the field. But then, I guess it was the whiskey I was drinking to ease the pain in my leg, I decided it would be a good idea to step it up and customize the model, and I arranged it where my last name would be stenciled on the back and my nickname, "Squid," would be stitched on the thumb. In my stupor, it looked cool, and soon I pulled out my credit card, entered my information, and hit send. Now, here is where things get murky. I don't know what happened next, maybe my finger hit the wrong button, but the website wouldn't take my card. It was something to do with my email address; I wasn't sure. But I couldn't turn back now. Nothing would be worse than a partially completed order where the money had left my bank, but no glove showing up at my house. I couldn't leave it suspended in cyberspace, especially given that the price tag was around $300. I had gone this far, so I might as well make sure I completed the purchase correctly. I entered a different email address and hit send again. This time it was accepted! Eventually, I fell asleep, pleased that I would finally have a glove I had coveted since I was ten years old, with my name plastered all over it.

Although I was still groggy when I woke up the next morning, I was blithely unaware of what I had done until I began to check my email and found a reply from Wilson Sporting Goods. Custom A2000 was in the subject line. The first line read, "Congratulations on your new custom Wilson A2000 glove!" And to make matters worse, there was not one email celebrating my new purchase, but there were two! *Both* orders had gone through. The realization washed over me like a fever, and I began to process the horror of what I had done. I had purchased the most expensive glove on the market and dared to put my name and nickname on it. How embarrassing would it be for everyone to see the worst guy on the team with the most expensive and customized model glove. I called Wilson and tried to inform them this had all been a mistake, and not only did I not want an A2000, but not a custom model and certainly not two. The flunky on the other end said, "Sorry, sir. Your order was custom and has already gone to the manufacturer."

So there I was, stuck with two custom Wilson A2000 gloves with my name *and* nickname stitched onto them. Plus, they said it would take about two months for them to arrive since it was custom. Perfect. Just in time for the season to be over. And that still left me with no glove for this year. A couple of weeks went by when I finally went to the sporting goods store and bought an excellent Rawlings model for $39.99, which has served me well ever since.

With Elliott gone and my Express team taking a break for a couple of weeks, I had a little time to sort out my new dilemma. Should I keep playing with the over-fifty team, or should I throw everything I had into the new team, of which there wasn't one yet? Should I forget the nightmare that was unfolding in front of my eyes and cut my losses, or stick around and make worse what was already a bad situation? Elliott would be back in a month, and then we start putting all our effort into our team. I was pondering those scenarios when the phone rang. It was Howard from the Playboys.

"Hey Jim, we are having a tournament in September, and we have an opening on September twelfth for a few teams. Are you interested?"

"Uh, I think so. Lemme check with Elliott." I was interested but knew perfectly well we had no team and no way to put one together because he was out of the country, but I figured a phone call couldn't hurt. If nothing else, it would let him know we were being thought of as a new team in the league, accelerating our discussions when he returned. I dialed his number, hoping to catch him while he enjoyed a bottle of wine with his wife amid an assortment of friends he had assembled at his villa in Tuscany. He answered.

"Hey, Howard from the Playboys called. He said they're having a tournament and have a spot for us if we want to take it. I know we don't have a team or anything yet, but I just wanted to let you know we might be getting calls like this, so we should get to work on the team when you get back."

"When is the tournament?"

"In September."

"Let's take it."

"But we don't have a team yet," I protested.

"Don't worry about it. We'll figure it out." I could almost hear the wine sloshing around in his glass amidst the music and laughter in the background.

"Uh, okay. But we don't . . . "

He had hung up. Despite my protests, it was on. We would play a game in three months, and we had no team. But that wasn't something that seemed to bother him, and despite it bothering me, I had complete faith in his belief that we could at least get nine guys on the field.

I called Howard back. "Uh, Howard. We'd be happy to take the spot!"

"Great. I'll pencil you in." I was about to hang up when he stopped me.

"Uh, just one thing."

'Yes . . . "

"What is the name of your team?"

Now, Elliott and I had kicked around a few names should we ever actually assemble a squad. He wanted to be called the Possums because he claimed we were old and sleepy. But I had been toying with an idea for a while. It had come to me when I was sitting at a stoplight on 15th Street in downtown Austin. There, in front of me, was exactly what was quintessentially Austin, a part of the city's lore, the very symbol of everything we wanted to be. It had been there all along, hiding in plain sight.

CHAPTER 9

END OF SOMETHING

You can be a kid as long as you want when you play baseball.
—Cal Ripken Jr.

Standing with Coach Cliff Gustafson, arguably the best college baseball coach of all time, with his arm around me about to call my name, was the most outstanding achievement of my life.

I knew at that point I had made the University of Texas baseball team, the defending national champions! I only had to listen for my name to be called, and it would be official. I could already imagine the backslaps and well-wishes I would get from everyone congratulating me on having the courage to go out and reach for glory! But as he slowly read the names of the players who would return to practice on Monday, a certain odd feeling came over me, and suddenly I was thrust back into the stands of my Little League, where my ears strained in vain to hear my name called when the All-Star teams were announced. He finished saying ten or fifteen names and told everyone else thanks for coming out. Once again, my name was not among them. He then took his arm from around my shoulder and walked away. I stood, for a moment, frozen. What had just happened? Did he make a mistake? I was incredulous.

But then reality set in, and I succumbed to the fact that not only had I not made the team, I had been cut, again. I snapped out of it and turned my way to the players who had actually made the team instead of just "thinking" they had and congratulated those I knew, especially Cisarik. I then strode around in a daze for a few minutes, trying to process what had just happened. It took another minute or two before I realized I would not be playing baseball for Texas. I would not be playing for anyone. I would be like everyone else, a college student. And as the sun dipped behind the clam shell roof at Disch-Falk, baseball, as I knew it from childhood, was over.

An exactitude comes with the understanding that something has ended in your life, although sometimes it can take a moment to register. It's like when a girlfriend breaks up with you. The first day, you are sure she will call you back, knowing she has made a mistake. Then a few days set in, and she doesn't call, and then you finally see her with her arm around one of your friends and it hits you. It's over. It's time to move on. That moment came a couple of weeks later when my astronomy professor told us a pop quiz was coming up, and I hadn't even begun to read the assignments. I understood clearly at that point I was no longer an aspiring baseball player; my baseball dream was over. I was like everyone else in my class, a freshman at a large university where other students were intent on doing well. At that point, I put my head down and hit the books, trying to put the sport in my past.

I had registered as a pre-law student after spending my senior year in high school reading about the careers of fascinating defense attorneys like Racehorse Haynes and F. Lee Bailey. Their storytelling skills are what drew me in. Impassioned pleas before a jury when the guilt or innocence of their client hung in doubt with all the cards stacked against them, and suddenly they pull the rug out from the other side's case. I felt I had a knack for that and imagined myself in a courtroom, arguing for the wrongfully accused, cross-examining a witness squirming under the glare of my probing inquisition. It seemed like something that could make for exciting days, like playing in Major League Baseball games.

But one day, the schoolboy dreams of faraway glory became rooted in the reality of my life when I found myself studying in the school law library and opened a legal textbook. I hadn't read more than a page or two when I realized I wanted no part. I could only make out about half the words. It was just one long Latin-sounding word followed by a Greek-sounding word, ultimately leading to a sentence that would double back on itself like a mountain road, going up, down, and nowhere at the same time. After shutting the book and erasing any ideas about being a lawyer, I marched to the admissions office and changed my major to undeclared. Soon, I was adrift in the typical flotsam and jetsam of being a first-year student at the University of Texas, attending classes in five-hundred-seat auditoriums, playing intramural sports, and praying how I would ever make it without baseball. But, miraculously, all my prayers were answered.

Since I had just turned eighteen, I was still considered of high school age. Finally, skipping the second grade was paying off, and my parents became the visionary forward thinkers I had always thought them to be. By being under nineteen, I was eligible to play American Legion baseball. American Legion was made up of high school players looking for a place to play but not yet ready for collegiate summer leagues. Lanier High in town had an incredible high school team in the regular season made up of many players I had played with at UHO. And the coach was looking for a few additional players to round out the squad.

John Reimer was legendary among high school baseball coaches in Texas, and he seemed to remember my name when I called to offer my services. He had coached Lanier High's perennial play-off contender, which consisted of many good friends including Dunnigan and Selber. I explained I knew he was looking for players and, yes, was already in college, but I convinced him I was still eligible to play. Reimer was a little reluctant (apparently, he still remembered how easily Dunnigan dispatched me at the plate two years ago). But, after a bit of cajoling, he invited me to play on his Legion team that summer. Instead of only Lanier players, we had some of the best in town from other schools like LBJ, Travis, and McCallum. The team roared through the schedule, traveling around the state and destroying opponents no matter where we went. The days and nights were filled with baseball and summertime fun and seemed innocent enough until we wound up in Texarkana, Texas, playing in the state championship tournament.

We won the first two games and earned a bye into the title game, so we had a day off. A few of us went to a nearby park, met a group of teenagers, and told them we were staying at a hotel in town for the tournament. Before we knew it, they had invited all their friends, and about thirty kids showed up in their trucks, loaded down with cases of beer. Reimer discovered the party, rounded us up, and went on a tirade. For some reason, he kept staring straight at me as if I was the cause, probably because

I was the only guy already in college, and he thought I was a drinker, which I wasn't (at the time). We still won the championship going away, but it seems like I didn't play much after that. And for the first time, it didn't seem to bother me. It was like a candle whose flame had begun to flicker. Thinking back on it, I must've understood way deep down it wasn't my team. I had asked to be on it and was just an afterthought rather than someone whom the team revolved around. The team was full of great high school players whose futures were still ahead of them. I was merely playing out the string, trying to keep the ritual of summer days, learned by rote in childhood, moving ever toward a goal that had long since vanished.

After winning the state championship, we flew to Memphis, Tennessee, where we met our first bit of tumult. We lost to a team from Kentucky but clawed our way back through the losers bracket to get to the semifinals, only to fall to a team from Tennessee. Once again, we were one win away from a chance to go to another World Series, the American Legion World Series. At least we got to fly home and didn't have to drive back through the night as we did in COLT League. Still, it was an amazing run, and for most of those teammates, it was on to college baseball and a new lease on life. For me, though, it was back to my sophomore year at Texas and no more baseball, I thought.

The mid-eighties began a new period for many people in Austin. The town was trying to stand up on its own legs as it transformed from a local state government and university town to a high-tech hub. For us, music populated the downtown scene with an endless supply of nightclubs with live acts playing every day of the week, and we tried to figure out where our future was headed, upside or down. We often would find ourselves at shows in and among the clubs along Sixth Street, where you could hear any type of music, from country to new wave or local favorites such as Joe King Carrasco and the Crowns. Beyond our burgeoning music scene, MTV now offered a continuous loop of bands with new sounds my friends and I were beginning to discover. Michael Jackson, U2, and Madonna were staples, and it seemed we spent more time in front of the TV than on a ballfield. Cable TV gave us even more reasons to avoid the sunlight and watch the endless number of college football and Major League Baseball games that began appearing on our screens. Going outside to find activities was no longer our routine, especially regarding organized sports. Where did I fit? Was I moving forward with the emerging new wave of musical energy in The Cure, New Order, and Tears for Fears, or being left behind with the likes of the Lawrence Welk Band? I wasn't always so sure. I felt like a dinosaur as I continued to seek baseball wherever I could find it. But that question would be answered next spring when I discovered a baseball team right under my nose while reading a bulletin board in one of the intramural offices (where I had a job as an umpire). It was a University of Texas club baseball team, and they were looking for players. One of my elementary school friends, who was also a student at UT, was on the team and said it had been fun. Thus, when the spring of my sophomore year rolled around, I showed up for tryouts. Club baseball didn't sound like much, but upon digging deeper, I realized there were plenty of guys like me. They had great high school careers but understood that a chance to attend the University of Texas and get an education would pay off much more than pursuing baseball at a small college. Some players were all-district, all-metro in Houston and Dallas, and even all-state. It was tailor-made for me, and not only did I make the team, but I wound up starting at second base. We played several small colleges around Austin, like Concordia and St. Edwards, and a few JCs from the Dallas area and various places around the state.

Looking back, I think I secretly harbored somewhere in the far recesses of my mind that Coach Gustafson would hear about this scrappy little second baseman on the club team and think I was what he needed on the varsity, but that never came about. It was enjoyable, but my lack of interest in baseball had begun to gather steam, and when the season was over, I decided I wouldn't play again while in school. Baseball didn't seem important anymore. It was the beginning of my questioning the validity of my earlier goals. Was I too comfortable continually seeking the familiarity of summer evenings watching red suns disappear behind dusty small-town backstops? Was it just a way to fill my days while trying to figure out what to do with my life? Perhaps it was because I no longer had anywhere to go with it, no higher level to reach, but when the season finished, I put my glove and spikes away and tried to focus as the finish line of my college education was starting to appear on the horizon.

CHAPTER 10
A LUCKY INTERN

Baseball is a universe as large as life itself, and therefore all things in life, whether good or bad, whether tragic or comic, fall within its domain.

—Paul Auster

After assuming I wasn't meant to be a lawyer, I had to figure out something to do, and the answer came one day when I ran into Spark while walking around campus. I asked him about his major, and he said he was trying to get into something called Broadcast Journalism. It was in the School of Communication and was called a Bachelor of Journalism, a B.J. I had no idea anything like this existed. He said it was designed for people who wanted to be on TV. Classes involved things like shooting videos and applying makeup, which sounded immensely better than Civil Procedure and Torts.

I asked him where to sign up, and he told me you couldn't just sign up; everybody wanted to be in it. You had to audition before a panel of professors and do a live newscast, among other forms of entrance gatekeeping. Initially, it seemed like there would only be a few people, and they would take most of us. I didn't realize that nearly two hundred students applied each semester, and the school only accepted twelve. It was a big deal, and if you didn't get in, you switched your major to something else. I don't know how we pulled it off, but somehow Spark and I were both accepted, and so that was it. I would use college to pursue a career in TV news. And if I were on TV, the only thing I was interested in talking about was sports.

Before I even started the actual curriculum, which wouldn't begin until the fall semester of my junior year, I visited the local NBC affiliate one night and knocked on the back door around ten forty-five. I knew the newscast had ended and thought a few people might still be hanging around. My goal was to meet the local sportscaster and ask him how I could become like him. His name was Vic Jacobs. Vic "The Brick" was fast becoming a local Austin icon. If he didn't like something in the world of sports, he would throw a little foam brick at the camera. It was TV gold, and I had watched him every night for the past year. After waiting a moment, suddenly, the door opened, and there he was, Vic Jacobs, with foundation makeup caked on his face an inch thick.

Here was a real television star back when the local anchor was an actual celebrity. He invited me in and couldn't have been nicer, sitting and talking for a half hour about how to break into the business and what being a local sports anchor was all about. As the conversation wound down, I got up enough nerve to ask if I could be an intern, figuring he would tell me there was an application process, but if he saw my name, he might put in a word for me. Instead, he said, sure, come on down in a couple of weeks, and I could help him with the sportscast and do all number of wonderful things. It was astonishing. An hour earlier,

I had simply hoped I could meet the guy, and now I was hired as his intern. In two weeks, I would begin my television career. All I had to do was show up at the station at the right time on the right day.

Of course, Vic was fired the next week, and no one knew who I was when I arrived at the front desk at my appointed time. Drew Speier, the weekend sports anchor at the time, was eventually promoted to the job. He turned out to be understanding and laughed when I told him Vic had said I could be an intern. He let me keep the job, though, and before I knew it, I was editing highlights and covering sporting events around town. They finally sent me to a high school football playoff in a town four hours away that would require using the station's news helicopter to get the highlights back before the evening broadcast.

Unfortunately, I was nursing a horrific hangover with a cold front rolling in that afternoon. If you have ever lived in Texas, you know that a blue norther can blow into town and drop the temperature from seventy-five degrees to freezing in minutes, with wind gusts reaching as high as fifty miles per hour. The day started nice and balmy, and I wore a short-sleeved shirt and a light jacket. When the copter hit the leading edge of the cold front, we bounced all over the place. The prelude to motion sickness began—sweating, wooziness, nausea—and as you might imagine, I threw up all over the only jacket I had.

Once we landed, I had no choice but to take it off as it was covered in the remains of my lunch from a local sandwich shop called Thundercloud Subs, and so there I stood, shivering for three hours in the stands. I had nothing more than a short-sleeved shirt to keep me warm as the temperature dropped and the wind kept howling, and what little bit of food I had eaten that day was in the trash can along with my jacket. I still got the highlights back to Drew in time somehow, and when he heard about my plight from the pilot, I think it sort of made him think a little more of me, and eventually, I had the run of the place.

From that point forward, I watched my interviews make it on to the sportscast and eventually was entrusted with editing stories that would air. I felt like I was a giant and knew that one day I would be on TV in Austin and be the king of everything great in the world. Unfortunately, there was still a little thing called experience that was necessary before being ready for the bright lights of Austin. So, it would be years before I could even hope to return to my hometown, which meant trudging out to small television markets and working my way back up.

CHAPTER 11
CENTRAL CASTING

The great thing about baseball is there's a crisis every day.
—Gabe Paul

Austin's moonlight towers, also known as moontowers, are iconic in every way. They are a staple of downtown Austin and have illuminated the night sky since being erected in the 1890s. History says they were designed to light the city after Austinites grew terrified upon discovering a serial killer. Austin was the first city in the US to have a serial killer. In the mid-1880s, a man chopped up several local women who lived in the servant quarters of some of Austin's more prominent residents. Books have been written about the subject. Legends have been told. One legend claims that the killer was never captured and that somehow he escaped. Apparently, he later turned up in London and became known as Jack the Ripper.

Until then, there had never been a killer in the United States who had attacked random people. But it happened in Austin, and soon after in London, so urban legend has it that it must've been the same person. Who really knows? The bottom line is the moonlight towers soon went up in Austin, presumably to quell the nerves of the anxious citizens. And in Austin, they have stood ever since.

Austin, by the way, is also one of the first cities in the US to have a mass murderer. In August of 1966, Charles Whitman shot and killed sixteen victims from a perch atop the University of Texas tower. Having gone to school there, I walked on the sidewalks underneath, going to and from classes, and was continually amazed at how far away some victims were when they were shot. You can still see the bullet holes in the walls under the tower.

As for the moontowers themselves, more than a dozen continue to work today, lighting the way for all of us below. They dot the landscape in various places, mainly in the downtown area. You might not even notice them if you didn't know they were there. They blend into the city's fabric and are often mistaken for cell towers. But for those who know Austin's history, understand its darker secrets, and have immersed ourselves in its culture, we know where they are and what they stand for.

The moonlight towers are treasures. Austin is the only city left in the world with working moontowers, which symbolize the city's past and present. They stood long before any current resident was born, and have segued into the city's future. They define us as a people, shining their light on others, and a perfect one-of-a-kind moniker for our team name.

"We'll be called the Moontowers," I told Howard as he waited for me to give him our team handle. I figured that he'd see the gravity of the moment, with the dawning of what would be a cultural touchstone in all our lives.

"Moontowers. Hmmm. Okay. (Non-plussed) I like it. I've got you in there. I'll send more details but be ready to play on September twelfth."

And just like that, the Austin Moontowers team was born, maybe not with the aplomb I was hoping for, but at least we were on our way. But the underlying problem still existed—we had no players. We also had no uniforms or anything resembling equipment. We didn't even have baseballs. And the first game was only ninety days away, and my partner was in Italy and wasn't getting back for another month.

And that's when the calls began. One after another, to anyone I could think of who could still throw a baseball. Forget about hitting; I needed warm bodies who could stand around until we could fashion a team in the way we wanted. Naturally, I looked first within our own set of friends. Having grown up in Austin, there were several pals from childhood or my teenage years still in the area. It wasn't as though we hadn't met anyone new; we just chose to stay affiliated with one another. We had gone from boyhood into the constant tumult of adolescence together through girlfriends, spring breaks, and high school hijinks. We were together when we eventually got married (and divorced), had children, and for some, grandchildren. And we are still there now as we knock on the door of becoming old men. So naturally, they were the first people I thought of as the calls went out.

I first dialed Greg Morisey, one of my oldest friends I had met in high school and who is generally regarded as the wisest among us, mainly due to his reluctance to involve himself in some of the more stupid antics of our youth. Greg, or G-Moe, or Modesta Sander, had been more of a basketball player in those days, but he was also a good golfer and fiery, and I was certain he would want to play on a team with his old friends. He had grown up in the same neighborhood as everyone else but spent his summers on his grandparents' farms, learning the ways of agriculture with the interminable booms and busts of the weather cycles. His way of thinking was methodical and balanced, so I figured he would at least give the idea some thought.

"No!" he said emphatically, almost shouting when I called him to ask. "No. I will not play. What are you guys thinking? You're gonna hurt yourselves. I can be a coach or something, but a player? Baseball? Uh . . . no." And since he was considered the most deliberate thinker among us, I had to stop and ponder what I was asking my friends to do. I was fifty-five years old, and I wanted them, some of whom were older than me, to come out and play hardball, against other men, despite knowing they had not thrown a ball or seen a pitch in nearly forty years. I had at least kept my baseball days going a few years after college. But many of these guys had stopped playing in high school, some even before that.

With that idea in mind, I scratched Moe's name off the list. I was 0-for-1. Not a good start, especially as I thought he would be a sure thing.

Next was John Sheeran, or "Johnny-D," the older brother of Spark. Both were tremendous athletes when we were young and had kept in good shape through the years. Spark was the first name to come to mind for the Moontowers but had recently moved to Chicago, so it was out of the question. I knew John would be interested, though. Plus, his son Jake had only a few years earlier been one of the area's top high school pitchers. A torn labrum in his shoulder derailed Jake's career, but he had been among the better pitchers in Round Rock, which produces its share of major league quality players, so I figured he'd want to play too.

"Of course, that sounds great," was John's response. I had only vaguely explained this was a baseball team Elliott and I were putting together, and we wouldn't play that often, careful to soften the toll it would take on the body. "Now, I'm sure you know," he said quickly, trying to qualify his ability, "I haven't played since I was thirteen."

"Well, honestly, no one cares about you," I interjected. The thing about old friends is there is no BS. You can shoot straight with them. "The only reason we are asking you is that we want Jake. We need pitching."

"Yeah, Jake will probably want to. 'Course, his arm is shot."

"This isn't the major leagues. We need someone who can get the ball over the plate."

"I'm sure he can do that," he responded confidently. "So, what is this again, a baseball team that plays once a month? On a sandlot?" He asked more questions I didn't have time for, but at least I knew I could count on both, which meant we now had four players, including myself and Elliott.

"I'll explain that later, but just get Jake, and I'll let you know when we get together for some BP."

"Is this hardba . . . " his voice trailed off as I hung up the phone. I knew we had him, and Jake would say yes too. There is something about a ballplayer whose career is cut short by an injury that will always say yes when asked to give it another go. It's a sickness. As for John, well, he generally didn't have anything better to do.

Next came Brian Vanek. Another friend from high school. He had been a skilled city-league shortstop, although in softball, but

I knew he could at least stop a grounder and perhaps get the ball moving toward first base. He said yes, as long as it didn't interfere with his fishing. I assured him it wouldn't (even though it was highly likely), and we were now at five players. Despite Greg's disinclination to play, we eventually landed just about everyone we had gone to high school with on the team.

However, neither Elliott nor I knew what two members of the group could bring to the table. Scott Malcom was a retired army colonel with an assortment of battlefield-related injuries. He was a helicopter pilot stationed in Europe and later served in the American wars in the Middle East. Mark Turner dealt in used cars. Neither was suited to be on the field as a player, but we knew they could serve as base coaches. One night I texted both and informed them we wanted them on the team, but perhaps we would use their talents somewhere other than on the field. Bingo. In! They knew their role and welcomed it.

We were getting closer to fielding an actual team but still didn't have anything that resembled the complex assortment of talents it would take to engineer a winning product. Beginning to imagine myself as something of a sports baron turned my attention to my neighborhood and contacted Ben Greene, although we called him Bennie Blades for no reason in particular. He was from Chicago but had lived in Austin for nearly ten years. A basketball player in college, he wasn't sure what he could do on the diamond but said he would be up to help. We needed someone we could depend on rather than a player of all-star caliber, so when he said yes, I was ecstatic.

The team began to slowly build. Elliott's son Austin, in college at Southern California University, would play if he was in town. My own son Alex would naturally be our catcher simply because he had at one point caught during his lifetime, albeit fifteen years ago. The key to this, I was slowly discovering, was to mix some of the old with some of the new, although the process was slow and without a discernible method. It was one by one, a phone call here, a chance meetup there, and somehow, someway, it took shape.

Elliott and I had agreed to meet when he returned from Italy and firm things up, as we were now inside two months until the September game. Nevertheless, on a blisteringly hot day in July, we grabbed a couple of beers at a downtown bar called the Mean Eyed Cat to discuss the makings of our burgeoning enterprise. He was overjoyed to hear about the success of getting at least the initial round of players signed up. However, he was still tethered to Howard's original idea of "casting" the team. He loved having the old friends, but he said it was time to create the roster with characters who could make it interesting on the field and off.

Not only would he look for players to play, but he wanted people who could contribute to the team's fortunes—designers, web specialists, influencers. He would uncover whatever it took to "cast" the team in the image we had discussed . . . a mixture of old and new Austin. And once he started phone calls of his own, the roster took off. By the July fourth holiday, we had the makings of a complete team straight out of proverbial "central casting."

Ryan Caruthers was one of the key "gets" for us. He worked with Elliott at Nike and was employed by IBM when Elliott contacted him. The discussion went something like this:

Elliott: "You ever play baseball?"

Caruthers: "When I was a kid."

Elliott: "Do you want to play baseball again?"

Caruthers: "That would be so awesome."

Elliott: "Good. You are chief designer for our team."

It was amazing how people fell into the vortex once Elliott talked with them. He had a Midas touch at whatever he put his finger on, and rounding up players was no different. One of the more exciting players to sign on was Cameron Duddy. Cam, or "Doc" as he liked to be called, is the bass player for the country band Midland. Lean and trim, with long graying hair and a mustache, he could've been a character from a Louis L'Amour novel. He sat with Elliott at a restaurant one night in Dripping Springs, a town outside of Austin and where the band calls home. There was whiskey involved, but I heard that at one point, Duddy was down in a crouch, showing Elliott how great of a catcher he had once been, and then he would spring up among the bar patrons and throw imaginary balls as if to second base. Who knows what really happened, but even if the story was only half true, Duddy fit the bill for what a Moontower should be and was precisely the type of player we wanted. And how Elliott described his fervor was exciting and made me think we were on to something that could be special.

The names soon began to roll in as quickly as I could add them to the roster. Sean Curran, who worked in marketing with one of the new local Austin companies called Ranch Rider, said yes. Then it was the CEO and founder of Tecovas, Paul Hedrick. Ben O'Meara, another marketing guru at the clothing outlet Huckberry, came aboard. Then we went back to the well with our old friend, Thomas Tyng, who was in Elliott's fraternity at TCU. Tyng had been Elliott's roommate in college, and I got to know him back then. I had kept in touch off and on through the years, but this team offered the chance for us to reunite, and our relationship picked up right where it had left off.

Chris Ellis, a former pitcher at TCU, said yes. I didn't know him until he joined the team. He pitched in college, and that gave me confidence we would at least field a team with some amount of experience. Then some of the new players began to bring in people they knew. Caruthers brought in a friend named Will Bryant, who turned out to be a nationally acclaimed artist. I was astonished at the depth and diversity of our roster. We had four sets of fathers and sons. We had players ranging from twenty-three to fifty-eight years old. We had tech guys, lawyers, musicians, artists, and everything in between. Some players had just moved to Austin, while others had lived there their entire lives. We had some who hadn't thrown a baseball in decades, and some who (after seeing them in our first scrimmage) had apparently *never* thrown a baseball, ever.

Ben O'Meara had at least played college baseball. He was from Maine, so he naturally became the Lobster. Sean Curran became known as Cowboy, perhaps for his propensity to wear a cowboy hat, but I sometimes think it was because he is more of an untamed spirit, akin to a cowboy from yesteryear. He reminded me of someone who might've lived in the Laurel Canyon area of 1960–70s Los Angeles, adventurous and free. I admired that quality about him. Everyone, it seems, was given a nickname, part of an initiation rite: Lobster, Legs, Boots, Counselor, Snake. We hired a young kid named Carter Blackwell to be our team photographer, although he had never shot baseball. Of course, his nickname was Shooter.

We were taking chances on people, not just because they came highly recommended by people we knew, but, more so than anything, because they were willing to take the chance on us. We had no idea what we were getting into, what we were doing, or how long it would last. All we knew now was that we had each other and were part of something called the Austin Moontowers. It was a real mix of the old and the new, just like the iconic moontowers themselves.

CHAPTER 12
PLAYBOY DEBUT

That's the beautiful things about baseball. You can be any size and be successful.

—Andrew Benintendi

Meanwhile, the Austin Express, my men's league baseball team, was doing well. They had opened the season with a string of wins, with which I had very little to do, and were in first place. So far, I had struck out twice, hit a couple of grounders, and dropped a fly ball. My knee was killing me, and I could barely put any weight on it, plus I was hitless in six at-bats. Still, I continued to show up and even scored a few runs here and there after reaching base by a walk. But increasingly, most of my time with this team going forward would be as the first-base coach.

Then something remarkable happened. Out of nowhere, I got a text from Howard. He said the Playboys were looking for a couple of players that Friday night at a field on the east side of town called Govalle Park. Govalle was where teams in the Austin sandlot league played many of their games. It was a city-operated field between some of the older homes and the new structures built as the city continued redefining itself. The field consisted of dugouts and a small set of stands. Behind the backstop was a dirt parking area. Simple, old, and with the right mixture of grit and soulfulness, it was a perfect setting for sandlot-style games. It was just that . . . a sandlot.

I told Howard that yes, I could play, and suddenly I realized that after a few short months, the original plan to play on the Playboys would be coming true. Of course, I knew that I was only a fill-in, but still, it was the Playboys, the team spearheading the entire sandlot movement. At this point, sandlot baseball was a storm rolling across the country, preparing to unleash its fury and I was just a grain of sand being swept along. I arrived at Govalle early . . . so early that only two other players were there. One of them was a guy who introduced himself as Northcutt.

Northcutt had been hanging around with the Playboys for several years, waiting for his chance to be asked to play. Instead, he catered for them as he was a restaurateur and owned a few spots in town, including Scholz's beer garden right near the University of Texas campus. Northcutt told me that after nearly *nine* years of waiting, Jack had finally offered him a spot on the team, and he jumped at the chance.

Eventually, the players arrived, filling up the dugout under the shade of the trees that lined a creek behind third base. I introduced myself, and we got to talking, and then soon more players showed up, including guys from the opponents that night, the Grackles. Then Jack Sanders arrived. I had never actually met him in person, so it was fun to say hello and tell him how much I appreciated what he had created. He said thank you, and we talked for a few minutes about how the Moontowers were shaping up; then, he said it was time to set the pregame into motion.

I thought the "pregame" would consist of a typical infield/outfield workout, but instead, Jack told us all to gather near the fence along the left-field line. Once we had moved into position, he explained that winning the pregame was maybe as important as winning the game itself. After a moment, he had us spread out, and the next thing I knew, I was in downward dog, and we were into a full-scale yoga-type routine. We stretched and moved and tried to twist ourselves into yoga positions, and I must say, I loosened up some, but there was nothing I could do about my knee. I kept hoping the pain and tightness would subside by stretching and loosening up, but it never did. Instead, I was perfectly limber enough for yoga, but couldn't run because of the knee.

Jack stuck me out in right field, which was probably the best place. During warm-up, he hit me a popup that, back in the day, I would've settled under and probably caught behind my back. Instead, I stood there for a while, misjudging the ball, and finally watched it land about five feet away with a thud. I sheepishly threw the ball back into the infield, at which point Jack yelled out, "Good Playboy instincts. Just let it drop so it can't do any damage." I laughed on the outside but inside, I was crying. I was awful.

I was now the kid who hoped the ball wouldn't come to him. And sure enough, in the second inning, a ball came my way, this time not in the air but bounding along the ground at about one mile an hour. By the time it got to me, it had nearly stopped. I bent down to field it like I had done a thousand times before, but about halfway into the bend, I realized that my knee wouldn't allow it. The ball rolled under my glove and picked up steam as it went to the outfield fence.

I turned around and loped it like a deer shot in one leg as if this was something I could recover from, but I knew I couldn't. I couldn't field a grounder. I couldn't catch a popup.

What was I doing out here? What was my purpose? At bat, I managed to eke out a bunt, whereupon Jack said slyly as I got back to the dugout, 'I like small ball." (A reference to Coach Gus's style of play, where hitters sacrificed at-bats to move runners over.) He was trying to make me feel better, but I knew this had gone about as poorly as one could've ever dreaded. After months of dreaming about playing for the Playboys, I had my chance, and sadly it was unforgettable, as in, we will never forget how bad this guy was and never call him again.

In my head, I wanted to blurt out an explanation about my bum knee, and that I was at one time an All-Central Texas star, and that at one time I had skills, and that at one time I had been *somebody!* But in the harsh reality of the here and now, all of that was gone. All that remained was the internal torture of knowing I wasn't somebody at all, not even in my own mind. All that matters in sports is what you can do on the field, and the hard truth was that I couldn't do anything. Not one thing.

CHAPTER 13
SPRING TRAINING

There are three types of baseball players—those who make it happen, those who watch it happen, and those who wonder what happens.

—Tommy Lasorda

As July turned into August, it was time to see what the Moontowers players could do. The best place was Howard's batting cage, so we invited the players we had so far to batting practice. Elliott and I huddled right before they got there, and we each took a deep breath, knowing this would be the true measure of our grand experiment. Would they like each other? Would they get along? Would they form cliques? Not everyone knew each other. I didn't know the players Elliott had recruited. I only knew the old high school buddies, so it would be eye-opening for me too.

It was interesting to see them trickle in. Most were carrying a glove (even though it was batting practice). Some wore tennis shoes. Maybe one or two had a bat. A couple of the more enterprising ones had a helmet. Handshakes were all around as players introduced themselves to each other. The team was off and running, and at least for the first few moments, it seemed to be going reasonably well. The conversation, awkward at first, began to flow more smoothly, especially once Ryan Caruthers appeared.

Caruthers was from a small town in East Texas and told me later that he knew he was different than the people he grew up with. That was apparent from the moment he arrived. It was as if he was shot out of a cannon. Tatted up from one end of his arm to the other, he was continuously beaming like a car headlight, and I could tell his genuine, bubbly attitude was bound to be infectious. Unguarded, he was prone to talking incessantly, then laughing at what he had just said, and although I never understood the jokes or references he made, it didn't matter. He possessed an intelligent mind, sharp and focused when faced with the many tasks we ultimately gave him. He had worked on some of the Jordan lines of sneakers while at Nike and would eventually spearhead our uniform design, and although I wasn't sure whether he was much of a ballplayer, that was no longer a concern. He had the spirit and energy that eventually would become the soul of the team.

At some point, it became time to turn on the pitching machine and see who could actually swing a bat, and that's when out of the corner of my eye, I saw him. He was trying to stay hidden in the back, but I caught him. It was Greg Morisey, G-Moe, Modesta Sander, the first person I called and the one who said he would only be a coach. Presumably, one of the other guys had talked to him about his decision not to play, or perhaps he had a case of FOMO (fear of missing out), but whatever the reason, he was in the cage, complete with a bat and helmet. And watching him swing the bat, I couldn't understand why initially he didn't want to play. His swing was smooth and natural, and he had talent. On his first cut, he drilled a pitch that, without the cage netting being in the way, would've found its way into the gap between left field and center. All the players were howling with encouragement. I instantly dubbed him Slugger McGoo as I had visions of him in the middle of the lineup, striking fear into the opposing pitcher, coming through with a clutch late-inning extra-base hit. All these things played out in my head for about two seconds until his second swing, when he pulled something in his back and went down like a shot.

For the other guys from high school, each swing looked painful, as if their arms were made of metal and badly needed WD-40. A couple of guys cried out when they swung. One bent over after his session as if he had just completed running a marathon, even though he hadn't moved at all. It was like watching a demolition derby, except no one was crashing into each other. I didn't have the heart to tell them we had set the machine to forty-five miles an hour, akin to Little League speed, but it was a start. The younger guys, honestly, weren't much better. I saw all manner of oddly assorted swings. There were hacks, blunders, and whiffs, but once everyone settled in, even the older guys, they found a rhythm, and no matter how ugly the swing was, they connected with the ball. And weirdly, it began to resemble a baseball team.

While watching everyone hit, Elliott told me to keep my eyes out for a player that Sean Curran said wanted to play. Sean told me his name was Marshall Newhouse. The name didn't mean anything to me, but when he showed up, stuffed into the cab of his 1972 Chevy C-10, I could tell he would be different from any of our other players. Newhouse stood six-foot-five and weighed 325, and when he introduced himself, it was clear why his nickname was "House." Later, I learned he had spent a career in the NFL as a left tackle blocking for the likes of Tom Brady, Eli Manning, and Aaron Rodgers. House explained that he wasn't retired from football but just waiting for the right opportunity. He had played in the playoffs the previous season with the Tennessee Titans, so it was not out of the question to think someone would call. But for now, he seemed intent on wanting to be a sandlot baseball player first and a left tackle in the NFL second.

I can only imagine the temperament it must take to be entrusted with guarding the backside of names like Brady, Rodgers, and Eli Manning in the NFL, with some of the league's nastiest players trying to get to them. Still, while visually imposing, Marshall is the most gentle spirit on the team, seeming to float among us. It would take going to a dark place, he later told me, in order to reach the level of violence required to play at that level. For now though, he was just another guy hoping to catch on with the team. He said he had played baseball while growing up in the Dallas–Fort Worth area and wanted to play again. We stuck him in the cage, and all gathered around to watch. I could tell he could play, and it didn't take more than four or five swings before he found his rhythm. And on the eighth swing, he sent a rocket back at the machine's electrical box, smashing it to bits. The House made the team and ended the practice in one fell swoop. The Moontowers were beginning to shine their light over the city of Austin!

CHAPTER 14

HELLO, GOODBYE

To me, baseball has always been a reflection of life. Like life, it adjusts. It survives everything.

—Willie Stargell

Getting your first job in TV back in the late eighties was not an enviable task. There were usually only two sports anchors at every television station, and it didn't matter how good you were, if there were no openings—there were no openings. So, if necessary, the employment search could take you all over the country. I wound up going to several interviews only to be told that I wasn't the right type or maybe with just a bit more experience, I might have a shot.

It was humbling in more ways than one, and meeting with the news director wasn't the only obstacle. You had to find out about the job opening and then hurry to get there before they had a chance to hire someone else. Once in East Texas, I had to change into my only suit in the bathroom stall of a roadside gas station. Urine covered the floor, and I didn't want my pants to get soaked in it, so I stood on top of my shoes and sort of hopped into my suit and dashed out the door before anything in the air could settle into my clothes. I didn't get that job.

After reading a *National Geographic* article one night about a "Middle Kingdom" on the West Coast, I decided to drive to every small market in the West, including the entire state of California. I set up meetings with news directors and dropped audition tapes off at television stations throughout California and Oregon. I remember driving down Highway 1 when suddenly it lay before me . . . the Middle Kingdom. It was the Central Coast of California, just south of Big Sur to Santa Barbara. Halfway between San Francisco and Los Angeles was the most beautiful stretch of land I had ever seen.

There was something about the light slanting across the sky, casting shades against the green and gold hills while the gray fog floated about the blue ocean. I would pull over and just marvel at the sight. There were stations in several small towns that dotted the coastline, and I tried everything I could to get inside the door of one. There was one little town that caught my eye in particular. It was called San Luis Obispo.

There was something about that little place, nestled among gentle hills just a few miles from Pismo Beach. I was very taken with it, and I vowed that if I could get a job there, I might stay forever. Nothing ever became of my efforts to get hired, though, and soon I wound up back in Texas, hunting for employment across the endless, dusty land when it finally happened.

A small station four hours away from Austin, in San Angelo, needed, gulp . . . a *news* anchor, not a sports anchor as I had hoped, but a news anchor. I interviewed with the news director on a Thursday morning, and by the time I had driven back to Austin, the message was waiting for me on my answering machine. I was being offered the chance to be the producer and anchor of the six o'clock news at KIDY-TV in San Angelo, Texas, one of the smallest markets in the country. I would make $4.00 an hour and needed to be there on Monday if I wanted the job. I immediately called back and accepted it. Never mind that I knew little about news; it was work. And one morning I packed my one sport coat, two pairs of slacks, and one pair of dress shoes into my 1969 Volkswagen convertible with the back floorboard missing and drove out there, ready to take on the world.

And it wouldn't be long before the world came knocking on my door. Within two months of taking the job, a little girl in a nearby town fell into a well. Suddenly, news organizations worldwide focused their coverage on Jessica McClure and a well in Midland, Texas, a city a couple of hours away. When I found out how close Midland was to San Angelo, I drove my little Volkswagen there with the top down, my camera and tripod sticking out of the back seat. Upon arriving, it was unlike anything I had ever seen before. There were lights and cameras and news anchors from all over the country, especially CNN, as this was the story that thrust that network into a worldwide phenomenon. I was standing right next to Ted Koppel while he was doing *Nightline*. The scene was surreal and eerie as the lights lit up the backyard of a small neighborhood, and hundreds of people milled around waiting for the rescue. I stayed through an entire night and then drove back with enough footage to put on my six o'clock show the next day. I didn't see Jessica emerge from the well, but I did notice an entire world of opportunity was out there, and I needed to be ready to be part of it.

Soon after that, it was Halloween, and I didn't know it then, but our producer was a budding makeup artist. Somehow the idea was floated that we should "dress" up in Halloween costumes and do the news. The San Angelo television market is not exactly New York, so there wasn't a lot of oversight as to what went on air. San Angelo sits in West Texas, at least a hundred miles from the nearest town, Abilene. There are only ranchers and cowboys out there. It is the closest you will get to living in the actual "Texas" you see in the old western movies. After careful consideration, it was decided I was to be made to look like a vampire, complete with a cape and blood dripping from my mouth. Our weatherman dressed up like the Hunchback of Notre Dame. We did the entire newscast dressed like that. Finally, for the last story, I broke into what I thought was a vampire accent only to have it sound more like Liberace with a head cold. The switchboard immediately lit up, and much to our surprise, everyone loved it. The old cowboys were yelling, "Ah want that ol' boy on my screen evah day!"

A few days later, I got a call from a news director in Abilene, an hour and a half away. He had heard from one of his reporters about a spirited young guy willing to drive his VW for two hours to get the story (or perhaps that he would do the news dressed as a vampire) and wanted to see if I might be interested in a job at his station. When he mentioned how much money I would make, I jumped at the chance. And so, less than four months after accepting my first offer, I was now working at station number two, this time as the weekend news anchor and making $6.00 an hour. I could now afford a second sport coat and another pair of pants. This was huge! In the two years I was in Abilene, I worked as the morning and weekend news anchors at two different stations. I was also a daily beat reporter, and although it wasn't sports, I was honing my storytelling skills.

At first, I sought out humorous, more lighthearted features, but with only five or six reporters on staff, everyone was required to cover the harrowing stories too. I started to enjoy digging up facts and finding details to build my nightly reports around; the juicier the story, the better. I owned the police beat, which meant I was looking for stories about crime and the goings-on at the local courthouse. In a way, it made up for my inability to seek a job as a trial lawyer and gave me a peek into a career I could've pursued if I had been more mature.

I covered a few sensational murder trials, one of which the defendant was sentenced to death. I interviewed family members upon learning their eighty-two-year-old mother had been murdered the night before during a home break-in. Perhaps the saddest moment was when my crew went with a search team trying to locate a missing ten-year-old girl. We discovered what turned out to be her remains in a field north of town, and I had the unfortunate task of being the first person to interview the girl's father just moments after he learned her fate. As he bravely tried to articulate his thoughts in this intimate moment, the lost look in his eyes left me feeling cold and distant, almost detached from myself.

I knew then that being a crime beat reporter was not what I wanted to do in the longterm; instead, I needed to focus on my original goal of finding a job in sports. I filled in for the sports anchors occasionally when they went on vacation and volunteered to cover games for them on my days off, all while trying to keep alive my hopes of landing one of those rare jobs. I put together a sports audition tape and sent it to stations from coast to coast looking for a sports anchor or reporter position, but for months heard nothing back. So, like in baseball, I focused on the craft of storytelling, trying to get a little better each day in hopes that something would come along.

While in Abilene, I had an unexpected day off. I was the weekend anchor, and there was no Saturday newscast due to the airing of a telethon. Therefore, I was free after I finished work on Friday, and drove to Austin to visit family and friends. I left around six that night, just me and my little VW convertible driving along the sparsely populated land between Abilene and Austin. I grew to enjoy that drive as it meandered between the plains of Abilene and the rolling terrain of Central Texas, barely scratching the edge of the Texas Hill Country. Bluffs near the edge of town broke up the flatness of the horizon. Abilene was an outpost with such a different feel than Austin that whenever I drove by those bluffs, I knew I was either entering or leaving something different in my life. I loved to drive with the top down and feel the wind in my hair. This night was in January and was chilly, so I put the windows up and the heater on and nestled into a comfortable slipstream while I drove.

About an hour and a half outside Abilene, I stopped for gas. I guess I wasn't paying attention to what I was doing, but I must've put diesel fuel in the 1969 gas tank. I didn't notice it at first, but after a few miles, the car started to emit a smell and began to sputter. It choked and coughed all the way to Austin. The little VW air-cooled engine trying in vain to dispel the diesel created a foul-smelling burnt exhaust that enveloped me in a cloud for the rest of the drive. I could've stopped at any point and wanted to many times. There were still two and a half hours of driving left through lonely roads on a chilly Friday night in January, but I was in no man's land. A trip back to Abilene would've taken just as long, so I pointed the car toward Austin and kept going forward into the blackness of the night.

For a while, I wasn't sure what my best move was, but I believe there is a cosmic energy in the universe, and whenever I can tap into that energy, my life seems to flow effortlessly. When I get out of whack, things have a way of breaking down. For whatever reason, despite everything that had happened and with the car choking to death, I felt an urgency to continue going. And as long as the car kept moving in the right direction, I felt like I needed to as well. Seemingly, against all known odds, I arrived about two hours later than I should've, but despite smelling like pure diesel fuel, at least I was home.

I stayed at my parent's house, and the next morning my dad came into my room and asked why I was there since I had never been home on the weekend after becoming an anchor. I told him about the telethon and that we had no newscast that day. He, almost disinterestedly, said okay and walked away. At first, I thought it was a strange reaction but didn't think much else about it again. Later, although I didn't need to be at the telethon that night, I decided to drive back to Abilene after visiting with my family and friends. We had been encouraged to assist at work if we could, so I joined my coworkers backstage, helping get the performers to where they were supposed to be. I escorted Shari Lewis and her puppet Lamb Chop to their spot. I ushered Lee Greenwood to the stage to perform another rendition of "God Bless The USA." If nothing else, the telethon broke the monotony of the never-ending weekend newscast and allowed a night for some cheer among the crew who worked at the station.

After the telethon, I went home that night and was asleep well after midnight when the phone rang. It was my family. They told me my dad had suffered a heart attack that evening and was gone. Just like that. It was all very matter of fact. Despite my protestations for more details, they said people were at the house to investigate; I should catch the first plane home, and they'd fill me in then. I hung up the phone and was in shock. I had seen him that morning, and he looked fine. I stared at the wall disbelieving what I had just heard. I fell over and held myself, sobbing uncontrollably while alternately gulping for air, thinking that I would wake from what I was certain was a nightmare, although I knew it wasn't. I was alone in a strange city, and my father had just died unexpectedly. It all happened instantly, and there was absolutely nothing I could do about it now except get home.

I called one of my coworkers, and he was kind enough to come and sit with me through the night as I tried to gather my thoughts. I mostly stared off into the distance, unsure of what was happening. I remembered when I was about eight or nine, the mother of a boy in our class died in a car accident. None of my classmates knew how to treat him when he returned to school. He was the first person we knew who didn't have a parent, and I often wondered what it must've been like for him. I can still see his eyes when he returned to school, with a faraway gaze as if something was happening somewhere where he could hear it but couldn't quite make out what it was. And now, here I was, without a parent too, most likely with the same faraway expression on my face.

I was only twenty-two, little more than a kid myself. Early the following day, I caught the first flight out of Abilene and made it home to Austin, and when I got there, my family told me the truth. He hadn't suffered a heart attack. He had committed suicide.

My mind went blank when they told me the news, and I grabbed my mother and hugged her while starting to cry hysterically, alternately heaving and bellowing with pain all over again. My entire family from San Antonio and all my aunts and uncles were there. I remember they sort of looked away and let me grieve. And when I had let it all out, they came up to me, one by one, hugged me and held me and comforted me, my mom, and my brother. I sat on our couch in the living room and tried to make sense of everything. No wonder he sort of looked at me weirdly that morning. No wonder he walked away, seemingly uninterested in my being there. I still couldn't quite comprehend what had happened. The only thing I was sure of was that he was gone.

My dad, listening to Johnny Cash on Sunday mornings on his Sony reel-to-reel tape player, wearing his white T-shirt, a relic from his military days. My dad, driving his step-side pickup truck, painted Columbia blue, the color of my high school, in honor of us. My dad, sitting with my relatives at family gatherings in San Antonio, while my mother danced without him, forever telling everyone, "I left my dancing shoes at home." He was gone, forever.

My mom and brother later shared facts and details about what had happened with me. He left a note that read, "I don't hurt anymore" on the kitchen counter. He then went into the garage, unhooked the garage opener, sat in his truck, and turned on the ignition. My mother had been out that evening, and when she couldn't get the garage door to work, she called my brother. My dad's truck was usually in the driveway, and it wasn't there, so she sensed something was wrong. My brother eventually arrived, and they got into the house where they found him. They decided to wait until I got home to tell me the truth. They wanted to spare me the shock, and I'm glad they did it that way.

Still, the suddenness and finality of the moment were difficult to unwrap. My brother took the news harder than I did, being four years older (twenty-six), living in Austin, and able to spend more time with our dad. He told me later that he was starting to understand him more, seeing him as a friend instead of the stern father figure he had been when we were kids. For me, though, he would become a memory permanently connected to my youth, when I seemed more concerned with my existence than his, something I have only recently begun to reconcile.

I stayed around the house to help with the funeral arrangements and see that my mother was okay. But after a week or so, I needed to get back to work and made my way back to Abilene. I remember it being cold and gray with a wind that continually blew from the north across the flatness and emptiness of West Texas. At the time, I simply started to drift aimlessly through my days and nights, usually alone and scared. I couldn't quite understand why Dad had done what he had. I felt guilty as if I should've known more, should've suspected something. My relationship with him was decent enough, but later, he became distant. Still, I never would've imagined something like this would happen. I was numb, confused, and out of sorts.

He took his own life, which came as a considerable shock. But looking back, it was apparent he was suffering from depression, although none of us knew it then. It's not like it is today. There were no awareness campaigns or outlets to reach out to, and none of us understood how to look for what would today be obvious symptoms. Depression runs in my family, and I am no stranger to it, but the ability to understand the signs and triggers has made it much more manageable. I am incredibly saddened we couldn't do more for him, and his loss continues to haunt me, especially how it occurred.

This is what I thought about, alone in my little house in Abilene, away from my family. I was just thankful my little car never gave out on me that night. It sputtered its way through the darkness to get me home. To see my father. One last time.

Finally, one day I got a call that would shake things up again, this time for the better.

A TV station on the Central Coast of California, the Hidden Kingdom, had seen my tape. They were looking for a sports anchor, and would I be interested in moving out there?

CHAPTER 15

PULLING TOGETHER

Baseball is about talent, hard work, and strategy. But at the deepest level, it's about love, integrity, and respect.

—Pat Gillick

We all felt terrible for House. He had probably always been the biggest kid in the class or on his team growing up and most likely broke things. He felt awful to have smashed the pitching machine to bits, but it was just one of those things that happened. It's hard to believe that in all the years Howard had run the batting cage, it hadn't happened before, but he said it was a first.

The next day Elliott wound up getting the machine fixed, or rather, replaced. He went to the local Academy Sporting Goods store and bought a new one. He told me he went back to the batting cage to drop it off, but Howard wasn't home. We had told Howard what happened and promised him we would make good on it, but so far hadn't told him we had a new machine for him. Elliott, in dropping it off, said he could hear his mother Jo's voice in the back of his head saying, "Always leave things how you found them." So, he took the machine home, cobbled together some tools, and sat down to configure it.

Elliott said he spent a good couple of hours trying to do it with no help, balancing the tripod legs of the machine while trying to screw the parts together. Eventually, he got it working and drove it back to Howard's house, where he set it inside the cage and took what was left of the broken machine, presumably destined for the trash heap, although I think he kept it around somewhere.

And so, the first big crisis of the Moontowers was averted. We knew we could hit, but now came the moment of truth: How would we play in the field? In the interest of self-preservation, I arranged a scrimmage against one of the other local teams, the South Austin Parakeets. Their coach, Nic Fowler, had been kind enough to meet with me on a Zoom call a few weeks before to discuss how the league operated and what I could expect as a new coach. We agreed to scrimmage at Govalle, where I had my awful debut with the Playboys.

Playing a game when you've been invited is one thing; arranging a game is another. It requires securing the field with the city, so I called the parks department and was guided through the reservation process by a kind and patient woman named Liz Tjachman. She and I got to know each other as I would continually fix each reservation to accommodate mistakes I would inevitably make, ensuring the proper date, the time needed, and, eventually, a credit card number. But, finally, things fell into place. At the agreed-upon time, I showed up with a few balls and a couple of new bats and helmets I had bought at Dick's Sporting Goods and waited for my "team" to arrive. And as with the previous batting practice, here they came, one by one, with various pieces of equipment, either newly purchased or found in the garage. The glare from some of the brand-new white cleats was almost as harsh as the setting sun behind the plate. If the cleats weren't brand-new looking, then the assortment of gloves was enough to marvel.

Some were found in attics or the dustbins of second-hand stores. Johnny-D bought a glove on Craigslist, which he later discovered had been painted over with shoe polish to cover its shoddy and weathered leather. It eventually fell apart. Watching them warm up, I was astounded at some of their forms. It was part comical, part horrific, yet wholly genuine. Despite the Bad News Bears aspect, I soon could hear the unmistakable sound of horsehide hitting leather and realized this was a team I was in charge of. And soon after an infield-outfield session that was more of an atrocity than a warm-up, we were ready to go.

I worked out a deal with the other team where we would play six outs. I didn't want to waste a lot of time with each team going on and off the field and was hoping to save my pitchers' arms so they didn't have to warm up between innings. That was a mistake from the word go. What began as a great idea went right out the window as the first inning turned into a slog, and I realized this team would take a little more work in molding than I had thought initially. I had let each player pick their position, as for many it was the first time I had either met them or seen them play baseball.

I had no idea what to expect, so I told them to go out and find a spot. Mistake number two. The players who should have been in the infield were in the outfield. I don't think any of the outfielders had seen a fly ball before, nor had they caught one. My first baseman, who was fifty-eight, declared that he could no

Getting a hit at University Hills Optimist. Thirteen years old and a mustache. Notice the polyester uniforms. *Photo courtesy of Jim Matthews.*

The Reagan High JV team. Elliott is third from right in the top row. I am right under him. Again, with a mustache. *Photo courtesy of Jim Matthews.*

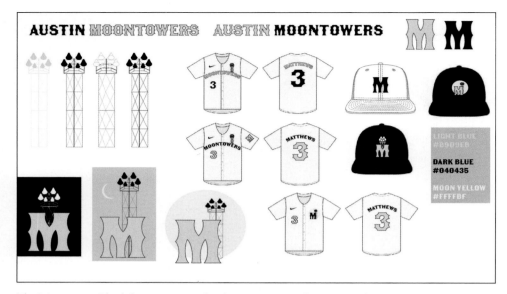

The Moontowers' look beginning to take shape. *Courtesy of Ryan Caruthers.*

An actual moontower preparing to shine its light on downtown Austin, the Capital of Texas, just as it has for more than a hundred years. *Photo courtesy of Jim Matthews.*

First practice featured gloves with more dirt in them than baseballs. Ben "Lobster" O'Meara trying to remember his college days as an infielder. *Photo courtesy of Carter Blackwell.*

Just minutes after meeting each other Ryan Caruthers, Will Bryant, and Cam "Doc" Duddy create the heartbeat of the team. Notice Duddy's outfit. The cut-offs are especially great. *Photo courtesy of Ryan Caruthers.*

The uniforms laid out just like in little league the night before the first game. *Photo courtesy of Carter Blackwell.*

The inaugural Austin Moontowers on opening day! *Photo courtesy of Kerri Megs Photography.*

Paul "Boots" Hedrick heading for the plate. Once he scored he seemed very much at peace. *Photo courtesy of Carter Blackwell.*

Elliott hugs me after scoring the first run in team history. "Can you believe it," he shouted, "You scored the first run!" *Photo courtesy of Carter Blackwell.*

The simplicity and beauty of the old time scoreboard at the Long Time where we still keep score by hand. PS: No one ever knows what it actually is. *Photo courtesy of Carter Blackwell.*

My favorite moment of each game: giving out the well-earned game ball! *Photo courtesy of Alex Street.*

Our tradition is singing the National Anthem acapella. They all try in their own individual way. It usually went horribly wrong. *Photo courtesy of Carter Blackwell.*

Nick from the Parakeets and Sean "Cowboy" Curran with a couple of canine supporters. "Spinach" is our unofficial mascot. He's deaf. *Photo courtesy of Carter Blackwell.*

A father celebrating his son's home run not as a coach or fan, but as a teammate. A fireball shot rounding third base became our ritual. *Photo courtesy of Carter Blackwell.*

Waco, a friend I have played ball with since we were ten, looks every bit as excited to make a play as he was back then. *Photo courtesy of Carter Blackwell.*

I'm certain Bennie Blades didn't remember his home run just two minutes later when he wound up taking shots on his teammate's lap. *Photo courtesy of Carter Blackwell.*

Marshall "House" Newhouse and Ryan "Legs" Caruthers showing why their thighs could just not be held in by thin polyester. *Photo courtesy of Carter Blackwell.*

The "Colonel" didn't get to play too much but he contributed in his own special way. *Photo courtesy of Carter Blackwell.*

Will Bryant touches home as the fans go wild either to celebrate us earning the home dugout or to simply watch a peanut run around the bases. *Photo courtesy of Carter Blackwell.*

The Moontowers finding some shade from the Texas sun between games of a doubleheader when the temperature reached close to 110 degrees. *Photo courtesy of Carter Blackwell.*

The Moontowers and Nashville Dollys exchange pregame gifts. This is a custom in sandlot baseball: create community and foster friendship from players all over the country. *Photo courtesy of Carter Blackwell.*

Will Bryant is an artist both off the field and on. Here he makes the greatest play in our short Moontower history, snaring a ball that was destined for the fence. *Photo courtesy of Alex Street.*

The Matthews boys getting a chance to play a meaningful baseball game for the first time ever as teammates. Andrew, Alex, and Papa. *Photo courtesy of Alex Street.*

The Moontowers and Dollys enjoying some post game camaraderie in front of the Moontower bus. *Photo courtesy of Liz Matthews.*

Four sets of fathers and sons. Alex and Jim Matthews, Austin and Elliott Hill, James and Thomas Tyng, and John and Jake Sheaeran. *Photo courtesy of Carter Blackwell.*

Your typical Moontower dugout features everything from drinks to photographers to gloves and, of course, some baseballs. *Photo courtesy of Carter Blackwell.*

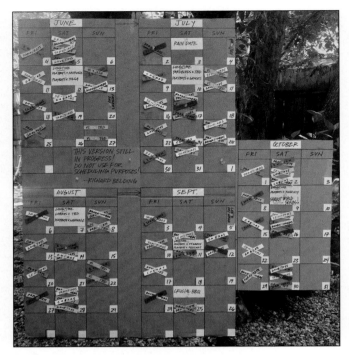

This is how we schedule games in the Austin Sandlot League. It is literally pin the tail on the donkey. *Photo courtesy of Jim Matthews*

Creating a family spirit means players of all sizes can enjoy each other. Our motto is to keep the game alive for those who may come after us. *Photo courtesy of Carter Blackwell.*

In New Orleans, where Austin Hill, James Tyng, and Chris Ellis enjoy a legendary Parkway Poboy. *Photo courtesy of Mike DiAlfonso.*

Some of the gang walking down Bourbon Street. Everyone thought we were on a "real" team and kept taking our photo. *Photo courtesy of Jim Matthews.*

Enjoying some time with the Gentilly Giants of the PBL in Hollygrove. *Photo courtesy of Liz Matthews.*

Jack Sanders, the one who started it all on his field of dreams. *Photo courtesy of Carter Blackwell.*

The Long Time is ground zero for teams all across America who want to share in the fun and spirit that has become Sandlot Baseball. *Photo courtesy of Jim Matthews.*

This is the crowd at the Moontowers-Playboys opening day game. It's a common sight at the Long Time, where people put down their phones and enjoy each other's company the way it was intended to be. *Photo courtesy of Carter Blackwell.*

Sugger McGoo, only moments before the home run that would cement our win over the Playboys, a dream come true. *Photo courtesy of Carter Blackwell.*

Elliott and me, co-founders of a team that became a family. *Photo courtesy of Carter Blackwell.*

Mark Turner, John Sheeran, and Casey Dunn congratulate Chris Ellis, who struck out the last hitter with the tying run on third base. It's the same smile they probably had when they were nine and ten years old. *Photo courtesy of Carter Blackwell.*

RYAN "LEGS" CARUTHERS   CENTER FIELD

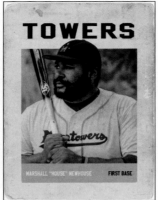

MARSHALL "HOUSE" NEWHOUSE   FIRST BASE

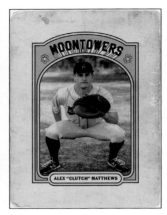

ALEX "CLUTCH" MATTHEWS

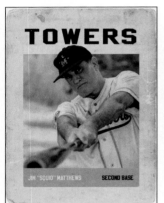

JIM "SQUID" MATTHEWS   SECOND BASE

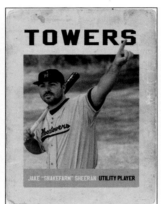

JAKE "SNAKEFARM" SHEERAN   UTILITY PLAYER

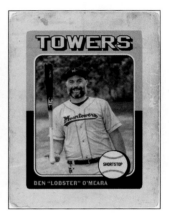

BEN "LOBSTER" O'MEARA   SHORTSTOP

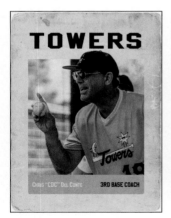

CHRIS "CDC" DEL CONTE   3RD BASE COACH

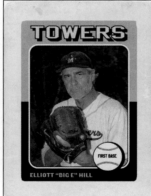

ELLIOTT "BIG E" HILL   FIRST BASE

PAUL "BOOTS" HEDRICK   BENCHWARMER

The Austin Moontowers. We hope you enjoyed the show! *Card photos courtesy of Kerri Megs Photography.*

longer see anything moving once it got inside ten feet from his face. And my pitchers, even the young ones, were laboring as each inning stretched interminably while we played one batted ball after another from a sure out into something resembling a tee-ball game. And then Duddy showed up.

Cameron Duddy's day job is as a musician. But he had grown up in an entertainment family and had been more of a video producer before focusing on music. He has won numerous awards for producing music videos for artists on the level of Bruno Mars, among others. Now, his band verged on stardom, touring the country on the strength of their album *The Last Resort*, performing in front of thousands every night. When he arrived, I asked him when he wanted to get behind the plate, as I understood from the story Elliott told me, when he said, "Oh, I'm not a catcher." Mistake number three.

But actually, it didn't matter where he played because all eyes were on his outfit. He was wearing Converse Chuck Taylor All Stars, cutoff jeans, blue-tinted sunglasses that looked like something Bono would have on, and a mesh hat that read NAPA across the front. He not only fit in immediately with the cast of characters we had put together but eventually became one of the most enthusiastic supporters of the team. Plus, he had good foot speed.

Unfortunately, the play on the field never got much better. I was of no value either, as I could barely run. I scraped together a couple of hits, and we were ahead for a brief period. But eventually, the score became a lot for them to a little for us, and I knew we'd have to do some rearranging if we wanted to be competitive. The idea in sandlot is not necessarily to win. There is no league championship. There is no trophy to hoist at the season's end.

But putting a competitive team on the field is essential to make sure it's fun for both teams as well as the fans.

Right now, though, I was happiest that everyone was finally together, and judging by the amount of beer drunk and the smiles on their faces, I could see they were like little kids again. It didn't matter that balls were bouncing off gloves and going over people's heads and between their legs. The only thing that mattered was they were excited to be playing baseball and, more critically, to be with each other. There was no sense of artifice or pretense. They allowed themselves to be vulnerable, and that vulnerability would eventually become the strength of the team.

We still had some time until the magical start date of September 12, and there was plenty to do off the field to keep us busy. I was learning in fits and starts what it took to get a game off the ground. First, one must find a team to play, make sure that the team wants to play you, and then arrange a date. You need an umpire. You need to let people know the location so they can attend, whether they are playing or going to watch. You must ensure your team knows how to get to the field. You must ensure you have equipment, balls and bats, helmets, and catcher gear, and all of that was up to me.

Elliott and I were developing our responsibilities organically as he had assumed more of a higher-level general manager–type role. He spent most of his time securing sponsorships and developing our philanthropic arm. I took care of the day-to-day tasks and was the coach on the field. In short, we did what we wanted and left what we didn't want to do to the other. It worked out perfectly for each of our skill sets, so, despite the looming date, most things had fallen into place. One thing I wanted was a team photo and individual pictures, like in Little League, where you hold the bat with a stupid grin. One of the top headshot photographers in the city agreed to take our photos at our first game so we could have one of our designers turn them into bubble gum cards.

We were getting close to Opening Day, and the roster was coming together. We added Bryan Barksdale, the general counsel of YETI, one of the homegrown Austin success stories in outdoor sports and recreation. Barksdale came to us through one of our high school friends. Their kids went to high school together, and Barksdale's son was a top-notch football and lacrosse player, so we were confident in his abilities. We also added Charles Attal, the owner and CEO of C3 Presents. Attal had become an instrumental player on the Austin and the national music scene. He was largely responsible for the growth and evolution of the Austin City Limits music festival and critical in developing the new Moody Center, where the University of Texas Longhorns basketball teams would play and Austin residents would enjoy concerts from major acts.

Meanwhile, Elliott had also dug into his extended network and reached back to one of his old friends. At one point, while at Nike, he was in charge of intercollegiate athletics, and since he went to college at TCU, he had become good friends with the athletic director there, Chris Del Conte, whom we called "CDC." Del Conte had since moved on to become the athletic director at the University of Texas. It was easily the highest profile you could have as a collegiate AD, and since Elliott and Del Conte now both lived in Austin, they rekindled their relationship and became morning walking buddies. During one walk, Elliott devised the plan to invite "CDC" to the Moontowers.

Del Conte's backstory is a unique one. He grew up in a children's home in New Mexico, but he wasn't a foster child. His parents ran the home with nearly thirty children living there off and on throughout the time he was growing up. During his formative years, he watched his parents provide structure and comfort for children in need. It served as the perfect training ground for becoming a "servant" leader of the nation's most extensive college sports program, handling the various boosters ranging from the youngest fans to the wealthiest donors.

I was amazed at how much Del Conte accommodated the UT family, helping to solve the most minor concerns of the burnt orange faithful (just follow him on Twitter). And so it was only natural that CDC would be a Moontower. At the time, I had no idea how much his personality would fit in with the team and propel the energy at our games, but when Elliott told me he was on board, I was thrilled.

As the roster was coming into full view, so was the schedule. Not only would we play a season opener, but we had added a few other games to the mix. We would play a combination of games at Govalle and the Long Time against teams such as the Austin Yardbirds and South Austin Parakeets. We would open up against the South Austin Lovejoys on the twelfth. The Lovejoys were coached by Wes Paparone, whom I met at the Long Time in May. He was a schoolteacher who had recently moved from New York and loved to play baseball. I had recently put together a team, and he had done the same just one year before, so both of us had navigated the inevitable pitfalls that came with the task. He was super helpful, and I was grateful our teams could square off in our first game.

Meanwhile, we had one more practice to get under our belts before the big day. We gathered at the West Austin Youth Association fields near where I lived. The league is better known as WAYA, and since the word *youth* is in the name, I should've probably known better. The sight of several middle-aged men taking over one of their game fields apparently didn't sit well with the league director. Before we could even take infield, a man appeared wearing an ear-piece and, with a glare in his eye, told us to get off the field. Even though it's a youth organization, it's not open to "youthful" adults who enjoy playing baseball and spreading goodwill.

This was the first time I had been kicked off a field for playing baseball since I was a teenager. When I was seventeen, about four or five of us, including Elliott, got into Disch-Falk and were hitting grounders to each other when Coach Gustafson appeared out of nowhere and told us to beat it. He was very friendly about it, although I still wonder how he knew we were there during the summer when no one was around. I almost told the guy at WAYA I had been kicked off better fields than this, but despite the moral contortions of whether we were in the wrong or not, I bit my tongue. Instead, we packed our cars, drove across the street, and took over a football field at O. Henry Middle School. We hit each other grounders and flies on the 40-yard line for about half an hour. People were running around the track that encircled the practice field when a grounder went through some-one's legs and was zeroing in on some runners. Somehow, the ball just missed catching them in mid-stride. It was a disaster averted, so we cut our losses and headed down the street to Deep Eddy Cabaret and the warm embrace of a few beers.

A week before the game, things started to fall into place as the alchemy of this group, many of whom were strangers less than sixty days ago, transformed into a team. Caruthers sent a video of himself throwing a baseball against a backstop. He was all alone on what looked like an elementary school field, throwing a ball repeatedly into the chain link fence. He would have to go get it, then run back about thirty feet and throw it again, almost as if he were playing fetch with himself. I sort of admired his determined, albeit inefficient, mode of practice. It reminded me of throwing the tennis ball against the wall in front of my house. Although in my game, the ball would bounce back. Still, he was giving everything he had.

Two days later though, less than a week before the game, Elliott called. He had been involved in a bike crash and had a concussion. It was enough I was fighting against time to ensure everything was in place, but now half of the leadership team was walking around in a haze. He told me he was calling while lying in a dark room. He had to whisper so his wife wouldn't catch him, as she had forbidden him to do anything other than rest. Then another player called and said he had COVID.

As the hours ticked down, it appeared things were beginning to spin out of control. Players were dropping one by one. One guy stopped responding to texts, and I had no way of knowing whether he was in or out. The uniforms arrived and were too tight on some and too big on others. One guy's head was too big for any of the hats to fit him. I was losing my grip a little bit and just needed a sign to tell me that things would be okay . . . anything I could point to for reassurance that the elixir had not worn off and this would not turn into an exercise in eating sand.

That sign came when we got a text on our team thread. It was Duddy. He informed everyone that he had bought his own pitching machine and was teaching his kids how to feed him pitches!

CHAPTER 16
HOME AND HOME

Baseball is like church. Many attend, few understand.
—Leo Durocher

When I walked into my TV station in Abilene and told my boss I was quitting, he asked, "Where are you going?"

"California," I said. Cali-freakin-fornia! The Central Coast! The Middle Kingdom of my dreams! I told him about my trip there two years ago and how enthralled I had become with the area. The CBS station in Santa Maria was looking for an eager weekend sports anchor and asked if I wanted to be their guy. A *sports* anchor?? I answered yes so quickly I don't even remember negotiating a salary of any kind. I just hung up the phone and called my family and friends to tell them I was headed into the setting sun of the Pacific Coast to begin my life as a sports anchor. It wasn't quite San Luis Obispo, but it was close enough, just a few miles away.

My boss must've sensed how excited I was, so he told me to leave that day; there was no need to come back. I gathered my things and shook hands around the newsroom and went flying out the door. I remember coworkers asking if I wanted a going away party, and I told them no—I was headed to California. I was afraid that if I stayed any longer in Texas, my new employer might just call and tell me I had gotten it all wrong. I packed up my car with everything I owned and began the trek across the empty miles of desert, heading in one direction, west!

As I drove toward the coast, I was filled with mixed emotions. It was nerve-racking to think I would shift from news to sports. Nearly two hundred candidates had applied for that job, and to get it was like being a first-round draft pick. People were clamoring not only to work in TV, but to be in sports, and to be in sports on the coast of California. And I was the lucky one.

Not only that, but I would assume a new identity. My mother's side of the family is Hispanic, and news directors had been telling me I should position myself as a minority since they were needed at that time in the broadcasting industry. So, as I drove through the desert of West Texas into New Mexico and Arizona, I left Jim Matthews behind. By the time I reached California, I was now . . . Jim Villarreal. It wasn't my name, but it was who I was. My family is Mexican, and I was proud to use their name. It was a little weird at first, but after a few weeks it became natural, and soon I was not only Jim Villarreal but a sports anchor too.

As I drove into California, I felt myself separating from the familiar. This was a journey into a new world. I dropped behind Los Angeles on Highway 101 near Calabasas and into Ventura. I could smell the ocean air, and as I drove along the water near Carpinteria and into Santa Barbara, I realized I was now in my actual TV market! I would be the one delivering the sports news to these residents.

I flipped around the radio dial and listened to Vin Scully, the legendary Dodgers announcer. The smoothness of his voice lulled me into a state of tranquility. The windows were down, and as I sped along the coastal highway toward the nothingness of the ocean sky, I could already sense that I was no longer further from home but moving closer to my destiny.

California, more than just a state, was a movie that had played on a continuous loop in my head while growing up in Texas. Its soundtrack was the songs of my youth. Groups like the Beach Boys and Eagles created a world in me where each day seemed endless and golden. And when I arrived, that was the world that indeed opened up—sun-kissed afternoons where endless waves lapped against the shores of Pismo or Avila Beach. Fog-drenched evenings rolled over the slopes of the Seven Sisters, extinct volcanoes from San Luis to the rock at Morro Bay.

After sunset, I'd venture into the deeper parts of California's soul, into the black contours of the nights. There, I connected to jazz music, preferring the cool sounds of Chet Baker and Stan Getz in Southern California and the piano of Vince Guaraldi from the Bay Area. I loved to read Jack Kerouac, whose books glorified Big Sur and San Francisco. I searched for the Beat Generation's enclaves on the city's side streets, spent hours in the City Lights bookstore, and traveled to the home where Neal Cassady lived in Los Gatos. And as I grew more familiar with the Central Coast, the smaller towns like Lompoc and Solvang, situated behind the hills that lined the 101, became familiar to me as I visited schools and communities and reported on their teams, learning the rudiments of polo and beach volleyball, sports that were foreign to a kid from Texas.

In the coming years, that Middle Kingdom drive up and down 101 became the most favorite drive in my life. Its twists and turns along that mysterious, almost fantastical patch of land among the hills always cast a spell on me. I made that drive hundreds of times, covering sports from Santa Barbara to San Luis Obispo. The green and gold land seemed pristine compared to the brown and dusty fields from my childhood. All the houses were stucco, white or painted lavender, pink, or green—not the brown brick or stone that made up most homes in Texas. I drove my convertible VW along the roads south of Santa Maria, across 154 or sometimes 246, through the Santa Ynez valley, past Lake Cachuma, and over the San Marcos pass before dropping down into Santa Barbara. The magnificence of the Pacific Ocean spread before me.

I thought about the cars my friends used to drive when we were in high school. Elliott drove a Cadillac Coupe de Ville with a landau top. It was nearly twenty feet long. Before I had my convertible VW, I drove a 1972 Monte Carlo, which was yellow with a black vinyl top. Spark drove some stupid Maverick with no matching tires. He broke off his gear shift at one point and had to stick a broom handle in the gearbox to get the car to move. My only contact with them from way out in California was an occasional letter or maybe a once-a-year trip back home.

Before email and texting was a thing, once you left a city or a town, you left that part of your life behind. California runs two hours behind Texas, and even when I thought about dialing someone to say hello, the timing would be off, and usually I wouldn't make the call. I was separated not only by the miles and the time difference but by the sense they were in my past. I had a family and a new career, and it was time to move on. My father's death had unwittingly signified a transition into adulthood. I could no longer rely on childhood friends. They were no longer there. I had to count on myself and my family and rethink where I was and where I was going.

After I started working in Santa Maria, I went to the Bay Area for a World Series game between San Francisco and Oakland. I wasn't officially on duty; I went as a fan. As I stepped out of my car at Candlestick Park, parked beyond the outfield in a dirt lot near the shore, I heard car alarms go off. I looked around, and suddenly my legs buckled underneath me. The earth rippled as a wave moved under the cars, bouncing them up and down, one after another. It was an earthquake. It wasn't just any earthquake but the Loma Prieta quake of 1989 that caused so much damage and loss of life.

Unbeknownst to us at the game, a section of the Bay Bridge that linked San Francisco to the other side of the bay collapsed along with a section of highway in Oakland. Death was everywhere. There was destruction in the Marina section as buildings fell and fires flashed. Debris and soot congested the air. The quake happened before the days of instant news, so for people in the stadium, there was no way to know what was going on outside.

Soon I found myself behind a CNN news crew waving at the camera when eventually, Gary Miller, the reporter, turned and asked me, "With all the bridges out, how do you plan on getting home tonight?" I had no way of knowing that bridges were down. I knew only that a World Series game was about to occur and I would be at that game. A bridge wasn't necessary to return to Santa Maria. I could just drive down the peninsula if I needed to. So, in my infinite wisdom, I came up with, "Look, it doesn't matter, just so long as we can come back and go to the game tomorrow . . . I'm in the south, though." Miller simply turned back to the camera and presumably the rest of the world and said, "Well, that's how it is with these Californians out here, they're kinda blasé about these sorts of things."

Of course, things were much worse than I had known, and once I understood the true measure of what happened, I made my way to KPIX-TV, the CBS affiliate. I filed reports back to my station, next to Susan Spencer, who was calling into Dan Rather at CBS News. I could see the fires roaring from the spots around town that had come crumbling down as the city literally rollicked and undulated, the earth eventually collapsing in on itself. The quake brought a unique reality that renewed over and over as the aftershocks set in.

I recall the rumble and the sway of the buildings, the city lilting and throbbing seemingly every hour on the hour as sirens wailed in the distance. I'm not sure where I slept that night. I just knew that this was the second time in two years I found myself inside a world news event as a reporter. And it would be another decade before I'd be front and center at the event of our lifetime. But in the meantime, I had sports to cover . . . and to play.

In 1991, I was asked to take over the weekend anchor job at the NBC station up the road from Santa Maria in San Luis Obispo. Though I would cover sports in the same market, the emphasis shifted slightly to San Luis Obispo and the surrounding areas. For many people, a move within the market was considered a lateral move, but for me, it was like reaching the mountaintop. San Luis Obispo was the little town I had fallen in love with from the magazine article and my trip to the Middle Kingdom. And there I was, a face and a prominent member of the community.

I loved covering all the high school programs, especially shooting high school football, then racing to put together my highlight package and doing live shots from the stadiums in nearby towns like Paso Robles, Atascadero, and Arroyo Grande. It was the heyday of my TV career, part performer, part informer.

One day, the main sports anchor got fired, and I was suddenly the sports director and lead anchor. So many years ago, I merely drove through, dropping off tapes. Now I was a local fixture in the community and could count myself among the many lucky people to call the Central Coast home.

As it turned out, Chris Del Conte lived in San Luis Obispo during the same years. When we first met a few months before he joined the Moontowers, I told him I was a friend of Elliott's. He had a quizzical look on his face and said he knew me from somewhere else but couldn't place it. After a while, the subject of San Luis Obispo came up. He suddenly lit up like a moontower and erupted, "I know who you are. You're Jim Villarreal!!! You're Jim Villarreal! I don't know you from Elliott! You're Jim Villarreal!"

He was beside himself. Before I knew it, he texted a group of former Cal Poly coaches who had been there when I was covering their teams and showed me to them on his phone. "Look who it is, it's Jim Villarreal!!"

After he calmed down, the story finally came out that while I had been a sports anchor in San Luis, he had been a fundraiser for Cal Poly, the local university I covered every night and hosted a coaches' show with their head football coach. Every week during the season, team functions consisted of Del Conte conducting mock interviews with players, coaches, and staff where he would pretend to be me, Jim Villarreal. "Hello everyone, this is Jim Villarreal coming to you live," he would say. It must've been a big hit with the team, although I never knew about it then. I wish I had known, but it makes for a hilarious story today. And to him, I am, and forever will be, Jim Villarreal.

While in San Luis, I joined the semi-pro team. I hadn't played baseball since my club days in college, and I knew my passion for the game was dying. I guess I thought that by playing, I could reignite the flame and make it burn again. But when I hit the home run, I knew the energy and the light had gone out completely. It's just how death is sometimes described when there is a moment of clarity in someone's eyes just before they succumb. When I rounded the bases, the flame extinguished, although it had burned brightly one last time before finally going dark.

During that period, I often thought about my father's death. Since then, things had become more serious. I had met the scepter of life and death in person, and it seemed the right time to leave my optimistic childhood template behind. Besides, I was inching away from baseball a little more each day. Growing up, it had been everything, providing benchmarks in my life. But in recent years, its controlling nature had become minimal, especially in California, where the game seemed far away. Doing what I did for a living allowed me more access to the sport than I ever imagined as a boy. I interviewed the Dodgers, Giants, A's, and other baseball greats, including my boyhood hero, Pete Rose. I was up close and personal with major leaguers and was in the locker rooms at Dodger Stadium and Candlestick Park.

But it wasn't the same. When I looked at the box scores, I did so for my sportscast. When I was around ballplayers, it was to ask them a question and then hurry off to put together my story.

Baseball wasn't something I let wash over me; it was just part of my profession.

And the importance I placed on it in my youth now seemed childish. Did a silly thing like baseball keep me from being aware? Was I too absorbed to see the signs of depression in my father? What would've happened had I known about his condition? What if I had asked him if he was okay? As I grew into an adult, I became more like him and wondered if I might follow in his steps. Deep down, I like to be alone and find comfort away from people. Would I suffer the same fate?

The conditions that outline life are usually based on simple rules. Grow up, get a job, have a family, grow old and die. For me, the signposts ahead always pointed in the same direction, but now there seemed to be a slight bend to the left and right. The path wasn't as straightforward as it once was. While in California, I was drifting, moving, floating, much like all the turns on Highway 101, passing beside the winegrowers of the Santa Ynez Valley and the surfers near Pismo. Baseball wasn't something I loved anymore. It wasn't something that I cared about or nurtured. And like a plant you forget to water, it died. Maybe it's called growth or change. I wasn't sure.

And then the strike of 1994 happened. There was no baseball from August that year into the postseason and no World Series. The game left me, so I left it—and turned my attention to other things.

On the other hand, San Luis Obispo provided me with a paradise. Every day was seventy-two degrees without a cloud in the sky; when it turned seventy-five, we all wondered what was going on with the weather. It was that way every single day. So why would I ever leave?

Well, one day another call came that would change my life. My old station, KXAN-TV in Austin, the place where I had been an intern, the place that had launched me into the world, the station in my hometown, was looking for a sports reporter. Would I like to interview for the job? Well, as you might imagine, I took the interview and got the job. In the summer of 1996, I headed back from my adopted hometown to my true hometown. I loaded up my little car with everything I owned and pointed myself in the opposite direction from seven years before.

So, on a foggy summer morning in July, I watched San Luis Obispo and the Middle Kingdom disappear in my rearview mirror and I cried. I was heading east, back across the desert from where I had once come. I was trekking homeward but leaving so much behind, including my name. Since I would be working in my hometown, I knew I couldn't go by Jim Villarreal, and would once more be Jim Matthews.

As I crossed into Texas, the reversal of my journey west before, I left a pair of boots at the state line. They were the last piece of clothing I took with me when I moved to the coast. I was coming home in a new skin, changed. In the poem "Paterson" by William Carlos Williams, he writes that "a man in himself is a city, beginning, seeking, achieving and concluding his life in ways which the aspects of a city may embody." Life altered the city inside me, and now I longed to see how my actual city, Austin, had transformed itself as I had in the seven years since I had left.

When I pulled into town, the temperature was 104 and thundering. I cried again. Little had changed there. But as I walked back into the station after being gone for nearly a decade, at least I felt a pang of familiarity, I knew the people and the sports, so it wasn't long before I settled into the job. The Texas Longhorns dominated the scene, and I became an insider to the sports program. I was standing in the end zone a few feet away when Ricky Williams broke the NCAA rushing record and was at the Downtown Athletic Club in New York City when he won the Heisman. I was there when John Mackovic was fired, Mack Brown came aboard, and Augie Garrido succeeded Cliff Gustafson. Augie would later win a pair of national championships, and I developed a friendly relationship with him as we spent several evenings downtown having a drink or two and ruminating on baseball and life.

Unfortunately, Texas wasn't as good as the team would become during the first few years when Augie was at the helm. The games at Disch-Falk were cold and dismal, and I dreaded going to the park as I remained wrapped in a blanket of malaise.

I became more interested in football and other sports I loved while growing up in the seventies. Austin's relationship with high school sports remained stable and strong, and it wasn't lost on me how the strength of high school football had moved from the inner city into the suburbs. Gone was the perennial state power of my school, Reagan, and in its wake was Westlake and, ultimately, Lake Travis, both schools pushing the boundaries of Austin ever westward toward the hills and beyond.

The late nineties were an exciting time to be in and around television sports in Austin as we welcomed a minor league hockey team, something unheard of in its day, especially as the sport grew to include several teams across West Texas. I loved working with my co-anchor Roger Wallace. The other members of the team were Ron Oliveira, Robert Hadlock, Jim Spencer, and Jim Swift, who became Austin icons. They were mentors and collaborators, especially Swift, whose style I admired. He shot and edited his stories, and I watched his process and modeled my own after him. I enjoyed editing and crafting the story from beginning to end almost as much as being on camera.

The fun the job created was endless, with each day naturally attuned to adventure. At one point, I covered the Dallas Cowboys, the team I had grown up idolizing. In those days, television reporters had to stand on the sidelines during the games at Texas Stadium, where the Cowboys played their home games, because there was no room in the press box. This was when Cowboys receiver Michael Irvin was arrested and outed as a cocaine addict by a reporter at KXAS-TV in Dallas named Marty Griffin. I must have resembled Mr. Griffin because while standing on the sidelines in the middle of a Sunday afternoon game, I saw a famous Dallas Cowboy eyeballing me. And soon Emmitt Smith, the league's all-time leader in rushing yards gained, walked up to me.

"Say, you're Marty, aren't you?" he asked with a serious look on his face.

"Uh, no. My name is James.

"No. You're Marty."

"No, I'm telling you my name is James."

During this conversation, the defense was on the field, and at any point, Emmitt could be summoned back into the game. But at this moment, his entire focus was on me. He continued with the inquisition. "I bet if I brought my teammates over here, you'd tell me your name is Marty."

"No, man, I'm telling you my name is James. Do you want to see my license?"

"Yeah, I think you're gonna have to show it to me."

So, in front of a national TV audience and sixty-five thousand fans in the stands, I reached into my wallet to pull out my license and handed it to him. He studied it for a moment, then gave it back.

"Okay, I guess you're James. But you sure look like this dude named Marty."

Despite the fun I had covering my former high school and college, and the Cowboys, I could sense a restlessness as the new century loomed. Eventually, in my deepest thoughts, I realized something wasn't right. Since I was in school, I worked virtually every weekend and holiday. As a sports anchor, when everyone is settling around their TV, I was off somewhere doing my job. Every Christmas, Thanksgiving, or New Year's Day, when families were together, I was somewhere else. If my sons had a game on a Thursday evening and needed a ride to practice, I was at work. I began to think of a career that allowed me to watch my kids grow up, coach their teams, and invest more time in their lives.

Television is a career that forces you to give up those things. I felt this singular pursuit of an objective had stunted my development as a person. And with my family growing and changing, this uncompromising drive to achieve in TV was no longer foremost on my mind. I wanted a lifestyle that made me complete and available, even if it didn't make me (at least in my mind) special.

And so, as the calendar turned from 1999 to 2000, I decided it was time to depart this profession. The question now was, what was I going to do? Worse yet, what was I even qualified to do?

CHAPTER 17

OPENING DAY

Baseball, it is said, is only a game. True. And the Grand Canyon is only a hole in Arizona. Not all holes, or games, are created equal.

—George F. Will

September 12, 2021

The first thing that happened was a fevered flurry of pings on my phone. A couple of hours before game time, Del Conte texted that he had to attend a celebration of the life of Arizona basketball coach Lute Olson. Then Attal texted, saying he wouldn't make it, although he eventually changed his mind. Another player texted. He had COVID. I felt like a shepherd whose flock, one by one, kept wandering away.

Still undaunted, my son Alex and I gathered up our things and headed to the Long Time, hoping to see at least seven other players dressed in some manner of the uniform that was carefully selected for the day.

I had my uniform laid out on my bed the night before. It was as if I was eight years old all over again, and this was my first-ever Little League game. It was exciting, and to know that I was driving out to the game with my son, who would take the field with me, was more joyful than I had imagined. It was the purest expression of baseball I could think of, father and son heading out to Opening Day. But instead of a father watching a son, it would be a father and a son taking the field together, which is indescribably fulfilling.

Upon arrival, though, the feel-good moment transformed into something of a military exercise as I took on the duties of a drill sergeant. Players arrived, asking me what to do and where to go and I maneuvered them to various places, handed out uniforms, and had them sign documents. I had arranged for a photographer to take our team photos and to shoot what eventually became our trading cards, so I quickly shuffled them over to a grove beyond third base where she had set up. Since we were playing at the Long Time, Jack Sanders brought waivers for us to sign, and I spent most of my time trying to round up everyone and get their signature.

Meanwhile, I could see everyone checking out each other's new uniforms. I hadn't seen them on anyone since Elliott first handed them out one evening after a practice. We gave each player two uniform pants, three jerseys, a couple of hats, two belts, and two pairs of socks. For this particular game, we wore our cream tops and bottoms with navy socks, belts, and caps. The team looked sharp, although a few had the wrong belt.

Once the photo session began, I could see them clustered in groups trying out their best stance for the individual pictures. Each player's personality came alive for this particular shot, and it was inspiring. Some looked steely-eyed into the camera; a couple tried to put the bat on their shoulders like Babe Ruth. Half of them always looked the wrong way and had to be redirected by the photographer. At first glance, it seemed like a disaster, but I could see they were having fun, and the photographer seemed to enjoy them. The bottom line was I could see the team was engaged and laughing, and the smiles were genuine. I couldn't wait to get on the field with them.

Finally, the first game ended, and we set up our headquarters in the visitors' dugout. The Long Time's dugout is sunken into the ground behind third base with a bench that runs the entire length behind (where all the drunks gathered, usually in the second inning, and stayed until the end of the game). Despite seeing the Long Time in so many videos and photos, it was surprising to get up close and be inside the backstop for the first time. The field was simple and made of the grass you might find in a typical Central Texas pasture with various odd bumps and bounces. The sliding pits near the bases were covered in dirt, creating an old-school Astroturf effect, where the entire infield was grass, and the only dirt was at the bases and home plate. The area behind home plate was deceiving as there was only about ten to twelve feet between the catcher and the backstop. Left field was deceptively close, and the net above the fence, designed to keep fly balls in the park, was barely beyond the shortstop. One ground rule stated that if you hit a home run from your original side of the plate, you had to turn around and bat from the other side for the rest of the game.

Our team lined up along the third-base line to get warm, and the players stretched from the outfield fence to the first-base line. Photographers and even a video crew were on hand. I remember warming up next to Duddy and listening to the photographer talk to him about growing up in California and how they were each into skateboarding as kids. I loved the team's diversity as I had played with kids from Austin or at least Texas for so many years. But this team comprised players from all over, with an assortment of life experiences, and I enjoyed their different takes on what we were experiencing together.

I was still nursing the knee issue and it was difficult to loosen up. I knew I would only play a couple of innings, so was more concerned with what happened before the game than anything during. I had rehearsed a short speech I would give once I corralled the players into a small group before the game. Butterflies like I hadn't felt in years zoomed around in my stomach. It was just a sandlot game, but this culmination of months of hard work was a defining moment for Elliott and me. I was nervous about how it would come off. Plus, we were playing at the Long Time, and an array of people had driven to this spot east of town to see what this new team called the Moontowers was about.

I wanted to make sure we would put on a good show, but I wasn't entirely sure how it would play out. Once we warmed up and gathered, I told the team that they were the original Moontowers and that would always stand. Players would come and go, and who knows how long it would last, but they were debuting as the inaugural team on this day and for all time's sake. And I told them how proud I was to be a part of the team and that when Elliott and I started with this experiment, we had no idea how it would turn out. To throw such disparate personalities together without a stated common goal except to have fun, and then turn them loose to see what happened . . . and now here they were, about to take the field in front of live fans and other players, it felt like something just short of perfection. We had a mix of personalities, athletes, and guys in it for fun. We had fans and supporters. We just needed to step in and make it all come to life.

Elliott added a speech in which he unveiled his sandlot philosophy: "Have fun. Be focused. Be fearless." The having fun was self-explanatory, but he wanted everyone to be focused because our oldies didn't move as quickly as they used to and we needed to focus on what we were doing each play. And to be fearless meant not worrying about getting hit or hurt; the sting wouldn't last too long. Once he was done, it was time to take the field.

We were the visitors and batted first, so when the ump declared, "Play Ball!" I ambled into the batter's box as the first Moontower to bat in a real live game. The Moontowers experience had begun. We were now part of the lexicon of sandlot baseball and the family of Austin sandlot teams. I had made out the lineups and inserted myself as the leadoff hitter. Since I was the coach, I might as well give myself the prime spot in the order, right?

The first pitch was low and outside and missed home plate by about two feet. Of course, I swung wildly and nearly fell over. I stepped out of the box and looked down to Mark Turner at third base, who had become engaged in a conversation with the third baseman and had no idea that I was even looking his way, so back in I went to work the count. It got to 3–2, and the next pitch was low and away. I tossed my bat and shuffled down to first base. I could hear all the players cheering and encouraging me as I became our first-ever runner.

It was surreal being out on the base path at the Long Time. I could see all the fans standing around and knew it was real life, but still seemed like a dream, much like what I experienced the first time I was there. But instead of watching what seemed like a movie, I was now part of the scene.

Another walk moved me to second base, and a grounder to short where the fielder couldn't make the play loaded the bases. The next thing I knew, I was standing at third base with my son Alex up to bat. I took an extra second to realize what was happening—my son was standing at the plate with me on third and a chance to score the first run in Austin Moontower history. It was quite a feeling, and I hoped that whatever happened, it wouldn't involve me having to make a mad dash for the plate.

My leg was hurting, and it took everything within me not to call for a pinch-runner. So, when Alex walked four pitches later and I strolled into home, I was astounded. Everyone cheered in the stands, and I could see the excited smiles on my teammates' faces as they swarmed around me. The Moontowers were on the board, and I was the person who scored the run.

Elliott grabbed and shook me as I walked away from the plate, yelling, "Squidly-Dee! Can you believe it? You scored the first run!!! You scored the first run!" We grinned at each other like a couple of eight-year-olds as if it was the first run we had ever scored in our lives. And in a way, it was. Never had my son knocked me in, and never had I scored the first run of a brand-new team in their first inning of existence. Sure, I had scored hundreds of runs with players from my neighborhood and my schools. And for the most part, they were all friends of mine. But this was different. We carefully selected these players to be part of this experience, and they were here . . . to make it memorable.

And it was. It was a moment that seemed suspended in time, and I understood the magnitude of what had happened. It tasted like sheer joy and lingered for a few more seconds, and then was gone. We were back in the game. Another hit and another run, but soon there were three outs, and it was time to take the field.

Everything that happened from then on was a blur. No balls came to me in the field, so I turned second base over to another player to more closely analyze what was happening in the dugout. I guess I didn't realize it because I was too wrapped up in my thoughts, but there was a full party going on! All the older players had found the wooden bench behind the dugout and were drinking beer and laughing. None had any clue as to what was going on in the game. They had played their "inning" and were now letting all the younger players come in for them. It was like a carnival.

Elliott was still in the game, though, and finally, it was his turn to bat. He told me before the game how nervous he was. His last time at bat was in 1982, when he was a senior in high school, thirty-nine years ago. I was excited and nervous for him because I knew just how much work he had put into making this happen. He had been out of town and landed at the airport with just thirty minutes to spare and had to race to the game. He dressed in the car just to make it on time. While he dug in, I remembered playing when we were in high school. We had spent countless days together on the diamond, just feet away from each other at first base and second, fielding ground balls and turning double plays. He was a good player but not the type who hit home runs, except in one game I'll never forget. He hit a blast way out into right-center field.

Back then, we played most of our games at Nelson Field near our school, which had a hill that ran up toward the right-field fence. His ball shot between the outfielders and rolled up that embankment. It would be an extra-base hit, no doubt about it. I can still see him tearing around second and digging for third. The outfielders were just reaching the ball, so the coach waved him toward home. Everyone on the team was out of the dugout and cheering him on; the fans were yelling when the throw came to the plate, and he scored standing up. An inside-the-park home run!!

We were hugging him and patting him on the back when the umpire strode right up to him, stuck his hand in his face, and bellowed above our racket, "You're out!" Our jubilation quickly turned to bewilderment. What happened? "You missed third base," spat out the ump. It was horrifying. Elliott had missed the base just as Spark had a few years before.

That thought went through my mind as he strode to the plate nearly forty years later. *Please let something good happen for him; he's earned it*, I silently implored.

Elliott swung at the first pitch; the ball hit the ground and bounded straight into the air. He broke out of the batter's box on his way to first base. When the ball came down, it hit him. He was out immediately. I could do nothing except slowly shake my head and smile. Our lives had come full circle.

The rest of the day was a menagerie of sunshine and a hazy mixture of late-summer baseball. We hit two home runs. Players made plays with their bare hands. At one point, no one could find our on-deck hitter. It turned out he was at the bar buying a drink. I saw my wife in the dugout talking to someone, only to discover later she was taking a beer order. Finally, it came time to get a team photo, which took place during the middle of an inning because that was the only time we could get everyone to pay attention.

The play of the game occurred later on when Paul Hedrick, the CEO of Tecovas, was at second base. A shot into right field seemed headed for the fence. Turner (who was wearing several sweatbands, a watch, and batting gloves as the third-base coach) waved him around. Hedrick told me before the game that he wasn't the most gifted athlete when he was younger. Yet, when he was digging for the plate, despite the gangly awkwardness of his form, it was the most determined effort I can remember in all my years in baseball. His fists pumped, his legs churned, and he crawled toward the plate almost suspended in time. His eyes were fixated on home, and his focus never wavered as he crossed the plate just ahead of the ball. It was magic, and a congregation formed around him, alternately cheering and clapping him on the back.

I returned to the dugout, and once all the cheering died, Hedrick came in and took off his helmet. I could see he was staring off into the distance, perhaps remembering when he was younger, and things on the sports field didn't go so well. But, on this day, at this moment, he had achieved. He didn't see me, but I watched him draw a deep breath with his chest puffed up, and then he let it out. He was a ballplayer on a baseball team. He looked very much at peace.

As for the rest of the game, we won somehow; who knows the score but win or lose, it didn't matter. It was all about the smiles and shouts of the wives and kids who screamed and cheered for their boyfriends, husbands, and dads. It was the first game *we* had ever played together. A new family was born.

After the game, a few of us went to Maudie's Mexican Restaurant along Lake Austin Boulevard for some margaritas. While sitting there, the political guru Karl Rove, an Austin resident, came by our table. He read our jerseys and exclaimed out loud, "Moontowers!! What are the Moontowers?"

Johnny D, drunk, garbled back, food spitting out of his mouth, "We are!"

I knew exactly what he meant.

CHAPTER 18
JOURNEY TO THE END?

Baseball is more than a game. It's like life played out on a field.
—Juliana Hatfield

In late 1999, while still working as a sports anchor and reporter, I met some people outside of television who convinced me that I'd be pretty good at public relations. I had worked with publicists daily for the last decade. Most were sports information directors, but they were all in public relations. And so, in March of 2000, I left the frenetic world of live television and entered into a new realm of working from nine to five Monday through Friday and seeing the world of storytelling from a different side.

I took a job with Corporate Technology Communications as a media specialist. CTC was based in Chicago and operated as a PR firm for various high-tech clients. It was the dot-com boom, and things were spinning quickly in Austin. Companies were popping up left and right, and everyone needed someone to deal with all the publications such as *Industry Standard* and *Fast Company*—magazines filled with content about the next big idea and advertisements bulging at the seams.

CTC had opened up an Austin office downtown, and I went from having a desk in the sports office at the TV station to having my *own* office on the fifteenth floor of a downtown high-rise. The view overlooked the hills of West Austin and beyond. I wouldn't say I had arrived because I was entering a world driven by the valuation of companies that had done little, but it was a beginning point.

Then, on March 10, 2000, a week before my first day, the NASDAQ tumbled. By March 17, the day I started, it began freefalling. A month later, the market officially began what is now known as the bursting of the dot-com bubble. It was probably best that I didn't have time to process how close to disaster I was. I was there for one reason and one reason only, to put my clients in touch with the media. Still, when companies shredded their staffs, and the industry magazines (for the ones who stayed in business) went from three hundred pages a month to barely more than a pamphlet, finding and placing stories was a little more than I bargained for. Still, it was a gratifying experience.

My boss was Rob Lanesey. Like me, he had once known the daily grind as a television sports anchor. He brought me into the world of public relations and taught me how to take my TV skills and exponentially increase them through an even more advanced art of storytelling. It was a skill second nature to us, albeit utilized in the finite format of TV news. After a few months of coaching, I slowly maneuvered through the myriad of roles as a public relations "expert," and soon began teaching executives and other team members the subtler concepts of communication. Eventually, Ketchum Public Relations, an international firm, bought the company, and I moved to a director position.

The lifestyle change suited me perfectly as I had more time to spend with my family, coaching my son's sports teams, and generally becoming used to weekends for myself. In it, I found the freedom to watch games from my couch instead of under the gun of a looming deadline. While exploring stories from the client's perspective, additional ideas and details could emerge and be fleshed out. There was no tremendous time pressure—no "Your story airs at 6:04 and it better be there." In public relations, the story had the opportunity to simmer and percolate, taking its time to reach the boiling point. Only then was it launched into the world.

But even as my corporate career was slowly taking off, my thoughts turned to being a purveyor of art. Real art. The kind of art you created by yourself. Not the type you pitched to others. And so, I tinkered with an idea festering since my days in San Luis Obispo.

I had always been interested in cameras and photography, and I got the bug of shooting my own video as a news reporter in Abilene. I ran with it even more in California as the sports world offered me a chance to be even more creative. I shot and edited my own video, wrote the story, and chose the music. Working with Jim Swift at KXAN in Austin further enhanced my skills as I saw how he crafted his stories. He also shot his video and created an entire movie, complete with a protagonist and a rise and fall of action, all wrapped into a minute and a half. I began to think of my stories that way and added music beds with quick and disjointed editing long before it became *de rigueur*. And I knew that if I ever needed to, I could produce and direct my own productions outside of the newsroom for a living.

While working in PR, I began to spend my weekends going to Little League baseball tournaments, shooting videos of the teams, and putting them to music. I hired a guitar player to create an original soundtrack and captured at least one action sequence of each player, and then edited it together to create a music video of the team. It was the modern equivalent of the old-fashioned team picture, except with moving parts. Parents bought the videos, and soon I had enough business to hire a couple of employees. I brought on board a hugely talented former sports anchor I met while working in Austin, and together we grew the business so much that it began to take up more than just weekends. Eventually, a change was the only option. Just three years into my fledgling PR career, I transitioned full-time into producing videos, commercials, documentaries, and eventually movies under the working name of my very own company, Slipstream Films.

Slipstream Films rented an office next to the Driskill Hotel off Sixth Street in downtown Austin, and there we set up shop, creating videos of anything that came in the door. Whether it was dog commercials for a local car dealer or working with celebrities like Paula Abdul, our company grew, and I honed my skills as a creative artist and source of my original talent. And as the production studio grew, so did another passion—making movies. I produced and directed short films and entered them into festivals. I even created a short documentary called *Dents Are Us* about a friend who owned a dent repair shop on Burnet Road in town while another friend sold used cars out of the front parking lot.

The two grew up together and were friends since high school. As business partners, however, they clashed. One was dedicated to his craft while the other played golf. I captured the uncoupling of their relationship in real time as the used car inventory was eventually repossessed, leaving the dent shop owner high and dry. It was an honest and forthright look at the interrelation of how much people play in our lives. No matter what happened in their professional relationship, it couldn't damage their years as friends. I entered it into festivals all over the country, and it fared well, winning a few awards here and there. The audiences genuinely seemed to gravitate to it, so I decided to try my hand at the big time by entering it into a film festival in New York City. I would feel like I "made it" if I could get the crusty New Yorkers to laugh at my lifelong friends deep in the heart of Texas.

And sure enough, when the lights went down at a small theater on E. 34th Street, I stood in the back with sweaty palms and a lump in my throat. I knew where the first laugh should come and waited nervously for that moment. When it hit, and a loud uproar came from the sold-out audience, I knew I had them. And soon, the laughs and guffaws from the crowd followed, and it was a hit.

I'll never forget standing in the back of the theater as they filed out, and when each person realized I was the director, they stopped and told me they couldn't believe these were "real" people. It felt like a coronation that my friends, the guys with whom I had come of age, could entertain the most demanding crowd there was—Big Apple filmgoers who possessed an acutely critical eye. I walked out of the theater feeling ten feet tall. I called my wife and told her how great the night had gone and that I'd be coming home the next day, but first would sightsee at the Twin Towers that morning. Then I'd catch the afternoon flight out of LaGuardia. I hung up with a feeling of triumph and celebrated with some of the other directors and festival attendees I had met. The date was September 10, 2001.

The following day I woke up in a fog. Everyone the night before had been in a congratulatory mood as *Dents Are Us* had such a great showing. At one point, I remember being at a bar underneath the Twin Towers, doubting I would make it the next morning to take a tour as the night was getting away from me. I returned to my rented brownstone on the Upper East Side and fell into a deep sleep. By the time I woke, it was already mid-morning, and the only thing I could think of was to concentrate on packing and not forget anything. I didn't dare turn on the TV for fear it would distract me.

Once I took a long shower and cleared the cobwebs, I gathered my bags and ventured out. My idea was to take a cab to the airport, eat something there and see if I could get an earlier flight. I reached the doorway and tried to exit just as another guy was walking in. He took one look at me and my luggage and asked in a slightly Australian-sounding accent, "Where are you going, mate?"

"Uh," struggling to formulate my first words of the day, "to the airport. I have a flight back home to Texas in a few hours."

"You're not going anywhere."

"What?"

"You're not going anywhere, mate. Haven't you seen the news?"

"No, what do you mean?"

"They've taken out the Twin Towers and the Pentagon."

"What? What do you mean *they've* taken out the Twin Towers?" By now, my face must've had such an incredulous look he gave up trying to explain anything.

"Why don't you go back in and turn on the telly, mate? You'll find out everything."

I went back to my room, thankful that my key was still working. I turned on the TV just in time to hear Tom Brokaw say, "There goes tower number one," and a moment later, "and there goes tower number two." I sat on the bed, dazed for about half an hour, unable to comprehend what was happening. I went to the window, looked outside, and saw the smoke in the air. Suddenly, it started to make sense; our country was under attack just blocks from where I was. I then remembered that the last thing I had told Liz was that I would be touring the Twin Towers that morning. She must be worried sick. I realized I hadn't even checked my phone in all the confusion of trying to pack. I couldn't get any service as it didn't seem like any calls were coming through or going out.

So I went outside to get better reception and walked to the corner of Madison Avenue at the end of my block. In this part of the city, things seemed normal. Traffic was moving as cars passed by. People were going about their business, walking their pets, and chatting on the stoops. I continued to walk and turned toward downtown.

After a couple of blocks, I could see the smoke drifting across and enveloping the city, an image that would become embedded in the minds of people across the globe. Finally, after about an hour of trying, I connected with Liz. She was hysterical and had been crying all morning. Upon hearing her voice, I was able to grasp the fear that gripped the nation and began to sob and heave at the thought of missing certain death had I been in the buildings as originally planned. Eventually, after a few minutes, we overcame our bewilderment, and she asked me when I would get home. I told her I had no idea. It seemed no one was getting off the island anytime soon.

After reassuring her I was okay, I tried to flag down a cab, but a black Lincoln pulled up and the driver told me to get in. I said I was looking for a rental car agency and explained my predicament. He told me not to bother. No one was leaving Manhattan for the foreseeable future. He then asked me if there was anywhere else I wanted to go. I couldn't think of anything else, so I said to take me to the Financial District. The news reporter in me wanted to see what was happening firsthand. He said he could drive me to a certain point, but they weren't letting any cars below Houston Street. Once we had gone as far as we could, I thanked him and tried to pay, but he said it was a national emergency and refused any money.

I jumped out of the car and entered Lower Manhattan as droves of people were leaving. It looked like something from a zombie movie. Every person was covered in ash, trudging forward in a slow, measured, inexorable march from downtown. A dazed, faraway look was present in each of their faces, with mouths opened almost as if still in shock. Along the sidewalks, people gathered around portable radios and listened to radio news broadcasts just as they might have when the moon landing happened. I stopped at a bar near Ground Zero for a bottle of water, and a man wearing a suit was shouting inaudible things at the television that played overhead. I nervously glanced at the bartender. We were the only three people in the establishment. The bartender pulled me aside and said, "Hey, don't worry about him. He's been here all morning. His brother was in one of the buildings, and he can't reach him on his phone." The shock of what had happened and the ongoing residual fallout set in at that moment.

I ventured back outside and continued toward Ground Zero. The crowds thinned as I got closer to the actual site. Soon I could walk almost an entire block passing no one. I was alone. Eventually, I was close enough to see the other buildings of the Trade Center still upright. Not more than a block or two from 7 World Trade Center (a third building which collapsed), hordes of people suddenly ran toward me with looks of sheer panic. And then I saw the unmistakable plume of smoke billowing from the street below, and the building simply vanished into thin air, falling in front of me with debris flying all around.

The building was "only" forty-five or fifty stories tall, and its collapse didn't have the impact of the other two skyscrapers. But watching an enormous structure like that fall to the ground a block in front of you is unsettling and unforgettable.

I eventually made my way to a plaza near the banks of the Hudson and, along with a crowd of other New Yorkers, continued to stare in the general direction of where the Twin Towers had been only hours before. Suddenly, someone ran past and told everyone to gather, so we did. He announced that a search crew was being assembled to go into the wreckage and look for survivors. As a group, we were to gather medical supplies, water, bandages . . . anything that could help when the wounded were brought out.

We jumped to the ready, and he paired us up. As only could happen in this sequence of events, I was coupled with a guy who introduced himself as Carlos, a cab driver from the Bronx. Our task was to find water and any gauze we could, so off we went, racing through various retail and convenience stores, asking for any goods they could spare. After about twenty to thirty minutes of combing, we came up with a few items and worked our way back to the plaza. Upon arrival, we noticed that little had transpired since we left. There were no makeshift hospitals or attendant medical stations as had been discussed. Everyone was standing around with their heads hung lower than they had been when I first arrived.

Someone asked what was going on. Weren't we supposed to be setting up a triage unit for the survivors due to arrive at any moment? Finally, someone whispered in a hushed tone, "There are no survivors."

After that, there didn't seem much reason to be there, glowering about in the brilliant sunshine of that September day. I'll always remember two things vividly—how clear and blue the sky was that day, so different from the skies in Texas. And those buildings that stood the night before. I had seen them with my own eyes, and suddenly they just weren't there anymore. And with their destruction came an end to a way of life we all had known. But those ideas were not yet in my mind as I trekked back toward midtown. I only captured the surreal quality of what I saw in real time. Cabs were harder to come by at that point, and the sun sank lower in the sky, casting shadows about the walled canyons. I ambled along Broadway, peeking in and out of restaurants and bars, but there seemed no sign of life anymore. All the people went home to be with their families or loved ones lamenting about the day's events. I had no one to cling to, so I worked my way up through what had become a ghost town.

At one point, I simply walked down the middle of the street. There were no cars, no people, and no law enforcement. New York had become a scene from an apocalypse, and I seemed its only survivor. Finally, I reached Times Square, walked right into the middle of the intersection, and marveled at what was occurring.

I was like Tom Cruise in *Vanilla Sky*, one person standing alone in the middle of Times Square with no one around. I felt alone and disoriented amid the closed shops and darkened windows lining Broadway. And without a family to return to, I eventually sought refuge in a nearby watering hole.

I sat down with a few of the other occupants staring blindly at the news on the TV screens above the bar that repeatedly showed the towers tumbling to the ground. Then the door swung open, and in walked an FDNY fireman. His clothes were thick with ash, and his expression was sorrowful and distant. He had blonde hair and a bushy mustache, and I could tell, even in his line of work, that he had been a man who had seen tragedy too many times. But on this day, he looked as if he had experienced something no one should ever see. He sat next to me, and I asked him if it was as bad as they said on the news. He just looked down at the ground for a moment and then slowly nodded, and I could see him reach with his hand and grab onto the bar railing to steady himself. At this point, the bartender walked over and stared at the fireman, looked right at him, and said in his toughest New York brogue, "Sir, you will never pay for a drink in this bar again."

Later that night, I again played the role of a reporter, calling in a live report to my old station, KXAN, in Austin. I tried to capture the sorrow of the moment but also the resolve of the New Yorkers who brushed off their shoulders the way proud people do and continued to carry on. I ended up staying in the city for a few days, spending time with some of the other directors I had befriended, all of us stranded together while the airlines worked things out. We spent hours drinking beers in the small bars of Brooklyn, alternately grieving but breathing, reaching deep inside when confronted with something beyond ourselves.

Eventually, I rented a car and drove to Philadelphia before finally getting a flight back to Austin. Liz took both boys out of school for the day to pick me up at the airport, each one leaping out of the car to hug me when I arrived. The intensity I felt in their embrace was a sober reminder of those who had been waiting at the airports across the country that day and would never hold their loved ones again. I had now been witness to two of the greatest disasters in my lifetime, the San Francisco earthquake and 9/11. Maybe those events triggered thoughts of my mortality, but it seemed time was moving quicker now, and perhaps there were other things I could accomplish while on the earth, the length of which becoming more uncertain with each day.

My production company continued to land new and different assignments, creating opportunities for me and the small group of people I worked with. But I also began to think outside of producing and directing. I got an agent and became an actor. I was mainly cast in commercials, most local but a few national spots. I even landed a role on *Friday Night Lights*, an Emmy Award–winning television show shot in Austin. I played the role of a college recruiter. After presenting the star running back, Smash, with a bag of boiled Georgia peanuts, I uttered the immortal line, "They're so good they'll make you wanna slap your grandma."

I also dabbled in comedy. My friend Dave Burleigh was a successful comic in California and was interested in creating a comedic duo. My role was to be the straight man. He told jokes, and I played guitar and occasionally sang a ditty or two. We played in small clubs up and down the West Coast from Monterey to San Francisco and even in Arizona. We were entertaining and found some success, but I realized that my budding comedy career was

169

probably not going to make it when, during a show on the campus of Stanford University, my pick got stuck in the body of the guitar. The show ended with Dave scowling and me trying to shake it loose, confidence and ego shattered.

And as an adult stripped of ego, however, there is an acknowledgment of a bigger picture. The urgency in the days grows, and the whims of youth are forgotten. As the decade of the aughts wound down, baseball, for me, had effectively died away and become something entirely of my past. But it wasn't the only part of my life that was gone. I sensed that something else was absent. I couldn't put my finger on it, but it bothered me for a few years. It started as a feeling I had forgotten something or left something of importance behind, and it gnawed at me.

For several months I was consumed with it, but it wouldn't completely rise to the surface where I could ponder what it meant. It was buried deep down as if I had repressed an important event in my life. And then, one day, it dawned on me. I had given up on one massive opportunity, and the idea of having unfinished business was not going away. It was now or never if I was going to do it. And so, after months of consideration, I made the leap . . . into law school.

CHAPTER 19
FATHERS AND SONS

Baseball is sunshine, green grass, fathers and sons, our rural past.

—Albert Theodore Powers

Part of being on a sandlot baseball team is not only playing baseball but trying to get people to come to watch you play. The idea is to create a mini "event" around each game so that fans can enjoy it and help build something meaningful. My wife, Liz, and I talked about it on many occasions. She had championed the team's idea from the outset and never once asked me if this was a quixotic quest to reimagine childhood or, worse, to right the wrongs of past mistakes.

Instead, she walked lockstep with me and helped enlighten me on building a brand and seeking out significant ideas other than using Diamond or Rawlings baseballs. We don't charge money for admission. We don't dance between innings. There is no pennant chase or league standings. Sandlot baseball is simply about getting out from behind the computer, getting off the phone and enjoying something outside, taking a three-hour commercial break from our busy lives and sharing it with others. Many teams try cookouts, food trucks, and musicians between innings for entertainment. Afterward, everyone from both teams can gather and get to know each other. That doesn't happen every time, but that is generally the blueprint for enjoying the sandlot experience. As Elliott put it, it's about building community. Consequently, that does mean getting on social media to promote your team.

Elliott and I opened our Instagram account a few days before our first game. I'll be the first to tell you I have very rudimentary skills, but I now am keenly aware of how giggly twelve-year-old girls must feel. Watching your followers grow is addicting. Will Bryant had over eighty thousand followers, and Cam Duddy had about sixty thousand. I had fifty on my account, most of whom were family or bots, with that number trending downward every day. The only rational thing to do was to turn over most of the IG duties to a younger player. It was interesting, though, that people would want to play on the team once we played our first game—and I had been warned about this.

Sure enough, one day later, the inquiries began via DM. I texted Nic Fowler of the South Austin Parakeets and asked him how to handle this. "And so it begins," was his reply. He cautioned that the team's integrity is based on the makeup of the personalities, so even though a guy had played college ball or was a former minor leaguer, the chemistry had to remain intact. He said the best thing would be to indicate the roster was packed (which it was) and invite them to come out and watch a game, maybe introduce themselves around and see if there was any symmetry with someone on the team. After each game, I got two or three requests a day. And it was flattering. I am happy that they thought enough of us to inquire, but our roster was set for the time being and with the number of guys on the team, playing time was already limited.

We not only had inquiries about joining the team, but many people had become enamored with our gear. I was constantly asked where to buy our Moontowers hats and jerseys. The beauty of sandlot is that it opens doors for so many people to contribute on so many levels. Designing uniforms, caps, and merchandise allows teams to do whatever they desire in terms of creating their "look." Some clubs wear jeans and maybe a T-shirt with a logo or a number. The Jardineros, one of Austin's early sandlot adopters, wear a green polo shirt and whatever baseball-type pants they might own. When Elliott and I first sat down to discuss our brand, we selected five players—Ryan Caruthers, Will Bryant, Sean Curran, Ben O'Meara, and Carter Blackwell—we deemed to be the design team.

They were responsible for the look and feel of the club, not only in terms of uniforms and hats but also in our website presence and other social media outlets. We even had baseball cards made up from the photographs we shot on Opening Day. It was like running a small company, and the fact that we had such innovative and successful people on the team, the possibilities were unlimited.

Like Caruthers, Will Bryant had grown up in East Texas and is a tremendous athlete. His sprinter speed is the reason we call him "Wheels." But despite his athletic talent, he realized in college that his creative side would be his life's guidepost. He is an immensely talented artist and utilized his skills to partner with small firms before opening his own design studio. He eventually landed jobs at major companies that grew from developing small ad campaigns to creating large-form art. Many of his murals can be seen at various places around Austin, including at the Austin FC soccer team stadium. His art, typically irregular shapes that he describes as positivity and color, appears, at first glance, simple, almost childlike. But upon closer viewing, the forms achieve an interconnectedness to each other as well as the space in between, a unifying gesture of goodwill. And there is very often a beautiful symmetry between art and sport. The childlike appeal of baseball, if viewed through a stronger lens, can reveal the layers and depths of bonds we, as adults, often struggle to achieve.

From his small studio in East Austin, Bryant helped to develop "Moon Man," the crescent-shaped character that adorns our blue "third" jersey, which became a big hit among everyone who has seen it. During our initial uniform discussions, Will commented to the entire team that perhaps we should wear the cool retro uniforms with the 1970s pullover V-neck jerseys. What he didn't know is that they weren't retro for me. We had to wear them growing up in the era of the horrifically bad taste of baseball unis. It was the years of polyester with the Sansabelt pants. I had longed my entire life to wear a button-down jersey with single piping on the sleeves, solid socks, and black cleats, as I had missed out on that style when it went out of favor just as I was getting into the game. So when, during the middle of a uniform design meeting, he exclaimed, "Wouldn't it be great to wear 1970s throwback jerseys?" I immediately yelled out, "NO!!! Please, God. No!!!"

He had no idea the depth of my despair. It was like PTSD. My entire life had been a hunt to wear the button-down look that had been the staple of major league uniforms from time immemorial. But baseball stopped wearing that uniform style when I was in Little League, and by the time it returned, I was out of the game. And now, I had the chance to create a uniform for my own team, in what would be the clarion call to high-level baseball fashion, and they wanted to ruin it with the V-neck pullover. Of course, I was voted down, and we eventually compromised and made the V-neck jersey our "third" jersey for special occasions. It turned out fantastic and is a credit to the design ability of Will and the team, but just slipping it over my head still gives me the shakes when I think back to putting on that type of jersey when I was a kid.

Before putting the group together, Elliott and I chose Columbia blue to be the team color as an homage to our high school. Earlier, my older son, Andrew, had developed an initial concept of how the logo and uniforms should look. He drew up a simple moontower from a photo he had seen and devised a goth-ic-style M for the front of the cap, harkening back to the 1890s era when the moontowers were initially installed in Austin. Once the designers got into the mix, the concept took off and became more than anything Elliott and I could have imagined.

The logo consisted of a silhouette of an actual moontower sur-rounded by a crescent moon and stars. That went onto a patch on the sleeve of our jerseys with Moontowers Baseball Club encircling it. The cap was navy with a Columbia blue letter M surrounded by the crescent moon and stars. We had a cream uniform with the word *Moontowers* in script across the front, a gray uniform with the gothic M on the chest, and the third jersey with Will's Moon Man character and a bat. Even our pants had a stitched "ATX" surrounded by the crescent and stars.

Each player was fiercely loyal to the team and dedicated to their craft. They took the design of the brand seriously and in new directions. All were much better than what either Elliott or

I could've done ourselves, and I was often left wondering what they were even talking about when we had meetings. Words like vector files, brand execution, schematics, peel lines, and applets would enter the discussion, and I would just tune out, knowing it had far surpassed my input. And this was just for the design of our helmet stickers. I usually contributed once the conversation became something like, "Boots and jorts are too much visually. It gets too clunky,"

"Yes," I added, "too clunky."

One crucial piece of our team beyond social media and uniforms is the father and son factor. We have four sets of fathers and sons on the team. There is me and my son Alex, who was twenty-eight years old (at the time of this writing) and our catcher. Elliott has his son, Austin, who is in his junior year at Southern California University. He only played part-time with us when he was in town, but he's a good athlete and was genuinely excited to be part of it. Thomas Tyng, Elliott's good friend from their fraternity days at TCU, played with his son James who had recently graduated from the University of Texas. He was our youngest player and our starting pitcher. He had pitched on a San Antonio Alamo Heights high school team that made it to the state championship game, so pitching for us was no big deal. He never seemed to even warm up, only appearing about five minutes before the game and striding out to the mound. Finally, there's Johnny D's son Jake. Jake's shoulder issues gave me a stomachache every time he pitched. He was our other starter and could bring the heat when he wanted, but I was constantly nervous watching him because I could tell he was reaching deep to see how far he could take it. And it didn't look to be the best idea for his shoulder.

Our second game, against the Texas Oil Dawgs, was the first time all the sons would be simultaneously on the field with the fathers. So, the eight of us, along with Lobster O'Meara, took the field together on a bright September Saturday. I can't explain the emotion I felt, but I'm sure all the other fathers shared it. It was a mix of pride, excitement, nervousness, and joy. At one point, I didn't want to mess up in front of my son, but I wanted something to be hit my way so we could enjoy the time together. Like most of the other fathers, I coached my son when he was growing up and had often been on the field with him. But this time was different. And only when the first batter hit a ground ball from James Tyng, who was pitching to his father Thomas at third, did I understand the connection. The action on the field operated as a bridge that connected two separate lives and combined them into one.

The next hitter launched a fly ball in Elliott's direction, and I could tell by his unsteady steps this could turn into an adventure. Elliott had wanted to play in the outfield, even though he was a first baseman by trade, simply so he could do the Ken Griffey Sr. and Jr. thing, where the father and son started in the same outfield in the major leagues. For now, though, the ball seemed suspended in the air while Elliott moved back, in, and back again. I could see, out of the corner of my eye, his son Austin, who was in center, looking skyward and then back at the fence, which was rapidly moving up to meet his father as he furiously backpedaled. When the ball began its descent, Austin started guiding his father like an air traffic controller helping land a 737. Elliott never lost his concentration, and just as he reached up with his glove, his backside made contact with a hay bale. The hay bales were decoration to give the field an old-time, old-school look,

177

and they achieved this effect remarkably. But for the unknowing, the hay bale was not something they would ordinarily expect in an outfield. I could see Elliott fall back into it, and just as he did, he lifted his glove about two inches higher, and the ball disappeared into the leather as he tumbled over backward, his feet up in the air and the rest of him disappearing behind the hay. A great roar went up from the crowd, and as I saw Austin reach in to pull him out, I knew the bridge had been completed. A father who had done so much for his son, but now, it was the son helping his father back to his feet somewhere on a sandlot baseball field in 2021.

I had my moment a few minutes later when a grounder took off between first and second. As I moved to my left, the ball took a big hop that brought it to about waist high and right into my glove. I had to make a quick throw to first, but the first baseman was in no man's land, and the throw nearly took his head off. In the distance, though, I could see little Tyng covering the bag as any good pitcher should, and the throw hit him right in the glove as he took two more steps and stepped on the base. It wasn't my son who caught it, but it was my friend's son, and that was good enough for me. In the grand scheme, a twenty- or thirty-year age difference between a parent and child doesn't matter. The shared moment together on the ballfield melds time in ways things like weddings and graduations cannot. It means the two souls are operating as one, which is probably how they were meant to in the first place.

The fathers could only last so long before giving way to age, so after two innings, it became just another baseball game. Duddy brought several bottles of his tequila company, Insolito, and things took a different turn once opened. The tequila flowed, and then Bryan Barksdale introduced Fireball into the mix. I can't be sure how this happened, but soon, the game no longer seemed important. Then, arms were thrown around shoulders, fist-bumps became hugs, and batters strode more confidently to the plate. The Fireball shots covered whatever the long-forgotten bravado and hubris of youth did not. And as we played on, Chris Del Conte, who had taken over as our resident third-base coach, suddenly asserted himself from the coaching box. The direction of his assault . . . the umpire.

"How can you make a call like that, Blue?"

"What game are you watching, Blue?"

"It's called Pearle Vision, Blue. Look into it!"

It was good-natured and all in fun, and judging by the umpire's response, he seemed to enjoy hearing every perceived slight just as much as Del Conte enjoyed dishing it out. Yet the onslaught was relentless. It was a nonstop running stream of commentary from the first pitch through the final out. More importantly, it gave the game much more meaning because once the other players saw he was having fun, they loosened up and realized our dugout was a no-judgment zone. They became free to express themselves in the innocent fun for which the game was intended. For Barksdale, it meant bringing the Fireball and keeping spirits light among the players. For Duddy, despite spending nights on stages across the world admired by fans of his band, it meant cheering for others instead of hearing the roars for himself, our very own carnival barker. His enthusiasm was contagious, and the players became fans of one other, with no one judging them for their ability or how they could help the team win, but rather how they could simply help the team. For Marshall Newhouse, for the first time in many years, it meant playing without throwing up due to his nerves and the unrelenting judgment that comes with millions of people watching your every move on a grand stage like the NFL. He could exist as himself on a small ballfield, with no expectations other than to enjoy the moment. I don't remember if we won or lost, but I know at the end of the game, we presented the Oil Dawgs with a bottle of Insolito. It's something they continue to talk about to this very day.

Before our next game, the pictures from Opening Day arrived, and they turned out just as ridiculous and honest as had been imagined. They looked just like the photos of major leaguer players that Selber and I used to see in the bubble gum cards at the flea market, albeit without the coating of dust. Great photographers can capture the essence of their subject, and ours did just that with the various personalities that made up the team. You can see it in a wry smile or a twinkle in someone's eye. You can also see it in how they wear their uniform or hold the bat.

It's funny, but people resolve themselves in adulthood. I compared my photograph with photos of myself when I was younger. In the early shots, I am not fully realized. Everything is still in front of me. But as an adult, most of my life has happened. There is plenty ahead, but the anticipation of what comes has been tempered by what has already occurred. In these photos taken on a ballfield, in a uniform, with a bat in hand, they captured not only the adult, more confident and secure, but also the imagined hopes and dreams that same face held a long time ago.

A few weeks later, we played the South Austin Parakeets. Before the game, they presented us with a poster they made for us, and we exchanged hats. Both teams sang the national anthem, as had become our new custom, off-key and a capella. As the game unfolded, though, something remarkable happened. Johnny D, fifty-eight years old, the eldest player on the team, got ahold of one, and it left the park. John quit playing baseball before high school, and although I knew he was a gifted athlete, I could only watch in stunned disbelief as he rounded the bases. John and his son Jake were part of the father-son combination. John coached him for many years and helped turn Jake into a high school star, so it was no secret that Jake possessed great talent. Sure enough, just minutes after his father's home run, Jake sent a pitch soaring over the fence. It was our team custom for the third-base coach to present the player who homered with a shot of Fireball when they rounded the bag. But when Jake rounded third, there was his father instead, to hand him his shot. For an entire lifetime, their relationship had been as father and son, coach and player, mentor and mentee. But after having homered in a ballgame together, and as John handed him his shot, they were no longer father and son; they were simply teammates, the transition complete.

By then, it became my routine to play an inning or two and hope that the ball didn't come my way. The knee was hurting badly, and lateral movement was impossible. I managed a couple of hits here and there and took my share of walks, but once on base, I usually called for someone to run for me. Besides, trying to manage things in the dugout was becoming increasingly more difficult as the guys got to know each other better, and the Fireball and tequila began to flow. A few of the older players, usually Slugger McGoo and Thomas Tyng, discovered they could start in the field, and once they played an inning, could hide from me the rest of the game to avoid having to go back out. They avoided eye contact when they knew I was trying to figure out who was supposed to be in the field. It was constant mayhem.

At one point, Sean Curran was supposed to be at bat and was nowhere in sight. I eventually found him in the parking lot, walking his dog. But, if he wasn't walking his dog, he was usually in center field with a beer, a cowboy hat, and maybe not wearing his jersey. Speaking of uniforms, Marshall and Caruthers had taken a pair of scissors to their uniform pants and now wore "shorts" to the game. Each proclaimed their thighs were just too thunderous to be held in by tight pieces of polyester.

Through it all, it was apparent the Moontowers were becoming something beyond just a baseball team. It was more of a community, the very thing Elliott had imagined from day one and worked tirelessly to promote, finding sponsors and raising money for others. We were both keenly aware of the world we moved in—seemingly without conflict and richly rewarded—and now we had the opportunity to create something where the journey could affect others in a thoughtful and fulfilling way. The reaction, and, more importantly, the team's sustainability, encountered unavoidable ebbs and flows, but for now, the foundation was sturdy and robust. Parents and grandparents were coming to the games. Children were watching their fathers, wives watching their husbands, perhaps with a new perspective than what they had before. I witnessed the respect we developed for each other, the players on the other teams, and the fans in the stands. It was not only the desire to play but the need for each other, camaraderie, and brotherhood; it was a need, perhaps more so than we originally thought.

Meanwhile, in the over-fifty league where I had begun the season, my team, the Express, won the season championship. I had been moonlighting the last few weekends playing with them in the playoffs on Saturdays and with the Moontowers on Sundays.

I didn't "play" much and had begged out of any actual competition, telling my coach I couldn't move anymore due to my
knee. I wasn't even there the day we won the title game and they
included my name at the bottom of the team photo, but it didn't
matter anymore. I had found the place where I was supposed to
be.

CHAPTER 20

LAW SCHOOL FOR DUMMIES

Baseball is almost the only orderly thing in a very unorderly world. If you get three strikes, even the best lawyer in the world can't get you off.

—Bill Veeck

The first thing I did in 2010 was go to a bookstore. I had always found comfort in bookstores, especially used ones. Selber and I whiled away many a summer afternoon huddled with books in the far reaches of the dusty used bookshops prevalent in Austin in those days. Today though, I was looking for a new book that perhaps held all the answers to the biggest question of my life. I was looking for *Law School for Dummies*.

After what turned out to be a year of soul-searching, I realized what it was that had been gnawing at me for so long. Becoming a lawyer was my original life goal. But after that fateful day in the University of Texas law library, opening a legal textbook and realizing my future was not to be found in its pages, I abandoned that idea and sought a different path. Even though my professional life had been fulfilling in TV, PR, and ultimately as a business owner producing and directing my own projects, the fact that I never completed the original quest bothered me.

So, after careful deliberation, I began to ask myself a series of questions. What if I went back to law school? I would be forty-four years old. It would take three years. Would I even be able to do it? What did I know about the law besides what I had gleaned from the books in my high school library? Was this just a pipe dream? Was I just deluding myself into believing I was making a career change? Or was it wasting time and avoiding success while chasing something that wasn't there? All these questions ran through my head as I wrestled with this notion.

I would be isolated and self-absorbed for three years. I had heard that law school brought out the worst in people, a monster that devoured all. And even worse, I had heard that nearly one-quarter of all lawyers developed drinking or drug problems due to stress. But it was a goal that hadn't been realized or, more sadly, even attempted. And above that, it was a culmination of all of my previous careers tied into one. Being a lawyer would be the ultimate storytelling job. People often ask how I moved from TV to law, but it has always been the same job—that of a storyteller. Whether I was going to an event and asking questions of different people and then reporting that information back to the viewers, crafting a commercial or corporate pitch, or now, telling a judge, jury, or opposing counsel my client's side of the story, it's all the same thing. I am giving a voice to those who cannot speak for themselves. And now the stakes would be magnified. It is one thing to get the score of a game wrong, but now my arguments would determine whether people would go to prison or whether the rights to their children would be terminated.

So that's how I found myself in the bookstore buying the *Dummies* book to begin my journey into the legal world. And quickly, I discovered just how dumb I was. The first thing I had to do was figure out how to take the admissions test. I studied daily, learning about logic games and reading comprehension, and the theory of deductive reasoning. I read books. I watched videos. I found myself in weird online forums for law school students discussing how best to approach the test. After three months, I drove to College Station and, with about two hundred other people, took the LSAT. It was a complete and utter disaster.

To begin with, I couldn't remember my ZIP code. It was the first time I had been required to fill in little bubbles on an answer sheet in almost three decades, and when it came time to fill in my ZIP code, my mind went blank. I had nothing. It was horrifying. And to make matters worse, due to my nerves, my stomach was making horrible noises like a cow stuck in a barbed wire fence. I know people who sat at least three tables away could hear that god-awful sound in the silent auditorium. Despite the fact I studied, I still couldn't recall anything I learned. It was as if my mind was a solid black wall. I might as well have been meditating. At one point, the proctor came to where I was sitting and discovered a piece of paper that had slipped out of my "clear belongings" case. I think it was my driver's license or something . . . either way, all it takes is one little distraction to throw you out of your rhythm, which is exactly what happened to me.

I didn't do well. Well, I didn't score as well as I had on the practice tests and a few months later, I retook it . . . this time on my old campus of the University of Texas in Austin. No brain farts, no proctors rummaging through my stuff. And sure enough, I did better. I had a good score. My application was complete. It was a matter now of deciding where I wanted to attend law school. Going out of state was out of the question as my son was a senior in high school, so I had to look closer to home. I sat in on classes at both the University of Texas and Baylor. Baylor, although a fine law school, probably the best in the state if you look solely at bar results, was just too young for me. Most of the students were right out of undergrad. Kids were passing notes in classes.

Texas, my alma mater, wasn't interested in me in the least. Quite honestly, they sent me my first rejection notice the same week I mailed in the application. It was like they had no use for what a middle-aged guy with a diverse background could offer. I was accepted to an Ivy League school, got a full ride from Ohio State, and scholarships from various other places, but not my alma mater.

I eventually found myself in San Antonio at St. Mary's University Law School. Although the school's reputation was not that of a top-tier institution, it had a night program for working adults. And it was there where I felt most at home. These were people who had been in wars, had loved and lost. They paid taxes and had been hired and fired. Many were former military people using their guaranteed government tuition money to pay for school at night while they continued to serve or worked on a second career. There were police officers, mothers, and architects. It was a potpourri of people. The diversity of well-informed opinions contrasted with the classes at other schools where most students were in their early twenties and had no view of the world. How could they if they hadn't lived in it yet? So, off to San Antonio I went.

San Antonio, Texas, is about ninety miles from Austin, and the drive down I-35 to get there is treacherous at best and death-defying at worst. And I had classes two nights a week. I thought about getting an apartment, but what good would it be for me to drive back to an apartment at night after class? I might as well go back to Austin. But if I could "walk" home after class, that would be different. So, at forty-four years old and having never lived on a college campus, I signed up to live in a dorm. Thankfully, it was an adult dorm more suited for professionals like me who simply needed a place to live.

The dislocation of living in a dorm at that age created more than a permanent strain; it required that I also do "back-to-school" shopping, which consisted of my wife going with me to Target to help pick out a bedspread, some hangers, and various other accouterments that any college student would need. Coincidentally, my son went off to college after my first year, so my wife was essentially shopping for back-to-school items for her son *and* her husband.

As the first semester wore on, I became accustomed to the cadence of law school, which consisted of reading all day, sometimes back home in Austin, then driving to San Antonio for class. The routine of reading, sometimes for eight to ten hours a day, and going to class at night became second nature, and I learned the real key to doing well was simply keeping up. Discipline is a rarer skill than talent, and I knew that by being disciplined, I could succeed, especially as there was nothing to do throughout the semester but read. There were no tests, no pop quizzes, and no assignments. It was just to read the endless number of cases and be prepared to discuss the material in class, especially through the Socratic method, where the professor probed your knowledge with a series of questions that could be answered depending on how the law applied to the facts.

The exams, on the other hand, were brutal. It was all or nothing—three hours with your entire semester riding on it. Most law school tests are about three or four questions covering the whole semester. Each question presents several legal concepts you need to spot and detail how each side would argue them. And St. Mary's was no everyone-gets-a-trophy school. We were graded on a very strict curve.

To my astonishment, I did well. I had several A's, and by the end of the year was the second-highest-ranked student in my class. When the top student transferred to Georgetown, I became the top-ranked student in a class of nearly three hundred. Naturally, that made the entire experience much more exhausting and tension-filled than was necessary. The following semesters I was not only in a frenzy about doing the best I could but trying to do the best in the entire class. I had nowhere to go but down, but I stuck in there, finishing three years later ranked eighth.

And as the semesters blended together, my questions started to get answered. Yes, I could do this. No, law school wasn't a fool's errand. Yes, becoming a lawyer could be a substantial and worthy endeavor. When I was younger, I had neither the maturity nor the discipline to endure something grueling like law school. But now, I looked back at my younger self and said, *You were right. A lawyer is what you can become. And should.*

While studying for hours on end, alone in my dorm room, my thoughts occasionally drifted back to baseball. I discovered a manager in the major leagues, Joe Maddon, with whom I felt a kinship. He seemingly did things his way, findings ways to win with a small-market team, the Tampa Bay Rays, who had a fraction of the payroll larger market teams like the Dodgers and Yankees had. He used the shift more than other managers at the time and had players play several positions. He was a breath of fresh air to Major League Baseball, and I began to notice him when he took the Rays to the World Series. And now, with nothing to do but sit and read by myself, I needed something to accompany me besides the hum of my dorm room air conditioner.

I began to watch the Rays games on MLB.TV on my computer. For a while, it was just to have some noise in the background, but the more I paid attention to the games, the more I began to believe in Maddon and how much he appreciated baseball and the limitless ways in which it can be played. He sought out the variables that others didn't see and put them in motion like a chess master, playing the game several moves ahead of everyone else, seemingly able to see what lurked just off the page. It reminded me of how I approached the game when I was younger, always trying to outsmart and outthink everyone since I knew I couldn't out-physical them due to my size. And slowly but surely, my interest in the game began to grow. It wasn't nearly like it had been, but at least it was something I could look forward to once I had come home from my classes, and there was nothing but me and a thick textbook to pass the time.

Many a night, I laid on top of my bed with a single light from the lamp above me trained on my book, while a few feet away, the sounds of the game provided the backdrop. It reminded me of when I was young and listened to games on the radio under my bedcovers at night. I hadn't fully bought in yet, but it was a start. Those Rays games sometimes were my only friend as I remained alone, locked in my room, studying the law and listening to a game from the other side of the country.

As for law school, three years later, in what seemed like the proverbial blink of an eye, I finished my classes and headed off to graduation. I walked across the stage with honors and could say I had achieved my goal of earning a law degree. Still, getting a JD is really like getting a degree in mistake-making. The learning curve is steep, and a degree only means more mistakes are coming your way. Hopefully, you make fewer and fewer as the years roll on, but I only had so many years left to figure it out. As someone who was closing in on fifty, I was simultaneously at the beginning and nearing the end of my career. In fact, after the close of the ceremony, I was stood amongst all my fellow graduates with my mom and my brother, who is just four years older than me, when one of them came up and said how glad they were to see that my grandparents had made it for my big day.

I became a criminal defense attorney almost by accident. Even though I initially had read about defense attorneys in high school, I wanted to be a prosecutor because they had more opportunities to be in trial. And I wanted to do just that, be in trials. Ever since I had read books about all those famous lawyers in high school, I wanted to be in the courtroom, bearing down on a witness and turning the case around. And the District Attorney's office was the best place for that to happen. DA's offices all over the country were always looking for new graduates to step in. Everybody was hiring, except in the one town where I lived: Austin.

When I passed the bar in 2013, Austin was experiencing a boom that has not let up since. Everyone was coming to town, to the tune of several hundred people a day. And more than a few of them were attorneys. Jobs in the DA's office were simply few or nonexistent. I cut my teeth during law school by working in prosecutor's offices in Austin and San Antonio. I even worked in the United States Attorney's office for the Western District of the State of Texas. By the time I graduated, I was ready to jump into a role as a prosecutor. But there were no roles to be found. I spoke with friends in the County Attorney's office and asked how their career path was going. They said it would take three to five years before they would handle trials independently. I was already forty-seven years old, to think I would wait until I was in my fifties to even get into a low-level traffic ticket trial. There was no way.

So, the path forward was carved out for me. I went into the world and became a defense attorney where I could handle my own cases and perhaps get into trial right off the bat. The only problem was, I didn't know how to be a defense attorney. I had worked for prosecutors during law school, and just because I had a bar card and a degree, I wasn't prepared to open a defense practice. Instead, I found out that a law school buddy was leaving a position in a small town near Austin called New Braunfels. He put in a good word for me, and eventually, I got the job. It was a little bit of everything, from criminal work to civil, divorces, wills and trusts, and even Child Protective Services. I got to do all kinds of cases and see many things, some involving the law and some not.

A few months after I started, I was in a very heated and contested hearing in front of a taciturn old judge. He was straight out of central casting and had the look and demeanor of a no-nonsense legal firebrand. And he was hard of hearing, so we had to wear lavalier microphones to broadcast our voices over the PA system throughout the courtroom. After a challenging back and forth between parties, my co-counsel and I went into the hall and began to speak in no glowing terms about the judge.

"Can you believe that?

"Yeah, what was that?"

"Man, he screwed us over on that objection."

"Yeah, that was a bunch of crap."

By then, we had made it into the bathroom and were standing in front of the stalls when the door opened, and the court bailiff walked in. He looked directly at me.

"Hey, man?"

"Yes?"

"Just wanted to let you know your mic is still on."

I had to summon every bit of courage I had, march back into that courtroom, and finish that hearing. I acted as if nothing had ever happened, and nothing was ever repeated about it. Although when I sat down, the attorney for the other side just smiled and shook her head. Despite all that, I still somehow won.

I worked for two women who were tough advocates and never let me get away with anything. I went with them to court, watched them argue tooth and nail for their clients, and learned how difficult it could be to become successful. One day, one of them came into my office and asked if I still had the Glock handgun I kept in my car. I told her I did, and she said I should get it. One of her divorce clients had just shot his wife thirteen times in the face with their child in the back seat. The wife died, and the killer was on the run . . . and the word was he was coming after the lawyer, who was my boss.

We buckled into the office while the federal marshals came over to protect us. Pretty soon, we peered out of the windows and saw various officers dressed inconspicuously in street clothes around the perimeter. At one point, my colleague with the raging client was no longer around. We thought she had gone home. Someone remarked that they would've gone home, too, if a deranged lunatic was gunning for her head. But after about half an hour, we went back to where her office was, and there she sat, having returned through the back door. I asked where she went, and she said she had gone back home. I then asked why she didn't stay home, and she replied that she had work to finish. And then she pulled out a .38 and a .45 from her purse, plopped them down on each side of her desk, and said, "I'll be just fine."

After a few hours, the phone rang, and it was the marshals. They said we could return to work, that everything had been "taken care of." When we asked what taken care of meant, they just said, "Don't worry about that, everything is cool." When I got home, I turned on the six o'clock news, and the lead story on all three stations out of Austin was the gunman had been killed in a shootout in a barn near New Braunfels.

My goal was to be on my own and in court by the time I was fifty, and I barely made it under that deadline. Three months before my fiftieth birthday, I finally got to do my first trial. It was a DWI case, and I defended a guy who had been pulled over and accused of acting strangely. The police said he had been arguing with the officers and was belligerent in the back seat. But there was no evidence of impaired driving, no evidence of his blood alcohol content, and no evidence from any breathalyzer. It was just the officer's word against ours. The jury chose our side. The most nerve-racking part was just before they read the verdict. My heart was beating as hard and faster than my client's. But when they said not guilty, he turned and shook my hand and thanked me profusely. He told me I saved his life since he was a commercial driver and would've lost his livelihood had he been found guilty. I wanted to say to him that I was honored he believed in me and that we still had a couple of post-trial matters to attend to, but before I could get the words out of my mouth, he was gone, out of the courtroom, and presumably back to his driving job. I never heard from him again.

After a year of covering cases of all types, I felt it was time to specialize. Doing so would require that I open a solo practice in Austin doing criminal and CPS defense. As you might imagine, this offered me a window into a world with which I was unfamiliar. The daily chaos of other people's lives was eye-opening as I realized that people were struggling with the exact details in life I take for granted. Yet, I found the journey, albeit strange, interesting and exciting, and settled into my job, appearing at court various times throughout the week, preparing for hearings, mediations, and trials. The rhythm and hum of the Travis County Courthouse became second nature, and I became immersed in the daily life of a solo practitioner doing criminal work as well as child welfare cases. I can only think that my previous careers, which involved dealing with the public in various forms, helped prepare me for handling people. So much of my life until this point, it seemed, had been focused on me. I wanted instead to showcase the lives of others and hope that my skills could enable them to have their voice heard. Nothing could prepare me for the factual situations in which I found myself.

I've dealt with parents selling their children for crack, telling me they would rather get high on meth than raise their four kids.

I've had single mothers with no means of income trying to parent thirteen children while being only thirty-two years old. I've had a convicted murderer threaten to kill me. I figured he didn't just talk the talk—he would do it, as he already had.

It is still storytelling, though. And in the legal realm, the story is even more vulnerable than in my past jobs, especially in trial. It plays out in real time, each word a moment of conception, like riding a wave. But, unlike a reporter, where the story glides along the surface, lawyers allow themselves to be battered by the wave. They sink to the bottom of the ocean and struggle for air before resurfacing to continue, gaining strength from the time underwater. I often read the summations of my favorite lawyers, many of whom I learned about back in high school. I find bits and pieces of their stories and try to merge them with the skills I've honed throughout my years as a live performer. I like to think I have the hubris necessary to pull it off, where I can be a philosopher and consider my transition from an artist into a thinker complete. But I would be lying. It is still an ongoing process, every moment of every day. Forever full of angst. It is just easier now to conceal.

And as the summer of 2021 presented me with many challenging cases, my personal life retook center stage. My favorite uncle died. Soon after, we had to put our dog, Willie Nelson, down. And a few weeks later, another uncle died. During this time, the Moontowers moved on from our opening game and gathered steam toward the rest of our schedule. And soon, my life's dichotomies would merge as I came to enjoy some of my very best days, while at the same time, enduring some of my very worst.

CHAPTER 21
LEGENDS OF SANDLOT

I've found the more you practice, the better you get.
—Ted Williams

As September turned to October, my Moontowers family got its first test when we scheduled a doubleheader. The first game of the doubleheader was against the vaunted Texas Playboys, a goal in and of itself, while the second game was against the team I believe was the best in the Austin area, the Yardbirds. This team was filled with a collection of former Round Rock high school baseball players. Round Rock was a baseball factory with a legendary coach and a program that had sent more than its fair share of players to the big leagues.

More important, however, was not just how we would fare against these two great teams but what would happen between games. Each game would be a four-inning affair, and we would play the opener and the nightcap. Between games, our team would sit for roughly two hours while the other teams played each other. A group of ballplayers playing for two hours, then sitting around for two more hours with nothing to do, could be disastrous. I lobbied to play the first and second games, but it just didn't work out that way. So, what would we do sitting there? Only time would tell.

Game 1

I arrived early, along with Waco (who was always early). Waco is a friend named David Monroe who, as the name suggests, lives in Waco. He and I grew up in the same neighborhood along with his sister Kerri. She had always been what I thought was the prettiest girl in our school, and Slugger McGoo wound up marrying her. David, equally as handsome as his sister was pretty, played sports either on my team or against me since we were ten years old. We attended junior high and high school together, so Kerri and David had been in my life for much of my childhood and a significant part of my adult years.

Interestingly enough, David started his career in television and worked at the same station in Abilene where I did. Later, he worked in Waco and was on hand to cover the Branch Davidian cult. He left the television business for greener pastures in pharmaceuticals and was now nearing retirement. Thus, with time on his hands, he regularly arrived with various tents, sound systems, and whatever assorted items we needed to put on a baseball game. This time he brought ant killer. Little mounds of ants dotted the infield at the Long Time, and it was becoming a hazard to slide.

When I arrived, Waco was out by second base pouring ant killer in the areas near the bases. Jack Sanders was also there, and I asked him about putting the poison on the field. He said to go for it. He was there early as well, and as I later discovered, he spent the entire weekend getting his field ready when he knew there would be a game. For him, it seemed almost spiritual—the ritual, the preparation, even just putting on the uniform. I felt the same way. I had been putting on the uniform and going through my pregame rituals since I was eight years old. Then for years, I didn't do it anymore, a way of life forgotten. But now, the sweetness of those moments returned, and if it happened to include taking out a few ants to make the sliding a little more accessible, then that was part of it, a rite of passage into the sandlot world.

I knew my action would be limited as my knee was so stiff I could barely jog. I was in great agony when I stared out at the mound as the leadoff hitter in the first game. Who did I see staring back for the Playboys? None other than Jack Sanders himself, in his trademark Stetson, red bandana, and jersey with the number 42, an homage to Jackie Robinson. I really couldn't quite conceive how far our team had come in such a short amount of time. It had only been a few months when Elliott and I were still trying to figure out how to contact him, and now here we were in a game with me standing at the plate facing the one who started it all, just sixty feet, six inches away from me. The Playboys had recently reached the lofty status of being featured in *Sports Illustrated*. The article featured hidden gems of fields, arenas, and courts around the country. Not only did the Long Time fit the bill, but it was enough to be the article's focal point.

His first pitch was probably no more than thirty miles an hour, and I swung so hard I twisted my knee into an even bigger knot and nearly fell. It was the "Purple Rain" pitch, what he is known for, a cross between an eephus (a pitch rarely seen anymore) and a slowball if such a thing is even possible. Either way, it came in as big as a balloon but was going so slow the bottom fell out from under it, causing unsuspecting players, such as myself, to wholly over-swing and turn their bodies into a pretzel in the batter's box. The second pitch wasn't much better, and this time I grounded out weakly back to him and simply carried the bat with me down to first base as I knew my day was done. The knee was hurting so bad I could barely bend over when a Playboys batter hit a ground ball in my direction. It bounced off the edge of my glove, and the runner reached base on the error. I knew I would only become a detriment to the team if I continued to play, so I pulled myself out when the inning was over and let Waco sub in for me at second.

This game proved to be a close battle, and the tension increased because we had to ump the game ourselves. Getting an ump can be quite a chore on Sundays, and that day proved to be no different. So, as sandlot agreements provide, the players call the game themselves from behind the mound when an ump cannot be found. Ryan Caruthers was quickly nominated for the post since he was dealing with an injury of his own and couldn't play.

The game went down to the final inning, with us leading by a run. As only could happen, the Playboys loaded the bases and scored the tying run. With the bases still loaded and two outs, a ground ball was hit to shortstop. Brian Vanek couldn't decide whether to go to second or first and chose a throw to second. The ball and runner arrived simultaneously at the bag. Caruthers hesitated for a second, then emphatically called the runner out. As we celebrated, a great furor arose from the Playboys, who insisted he was safe. Both benches came out of the dugout, and there was a lot of milling around as players on both teams pled their cases.

At some point, Caruthers decided to change his call. By this time, since the bases had been loaded, the safe call meant the runner had scored, and the Playboys won. Of course, in sandlot baseball, often no one is keeping score, so Jack didn't know the call meant his team had won. He thought it meant the game was tied. When I informed him the change in the call had inadvertently given his team a victory, he declared, "No! The Playboys will not win this way. We will revert to what the score was before." After a moment to mull it over, it was decided at the game would end in a tie. It was all fun, and there was a good-natured, if not hilarious, tone to the arguments. Most of the players were drunk and had a difficult time trying to piece together coherent sentences. For the very few that could articulate their points, most overlooked the facts and what was argued resembled the actual events in time and location only.

Eventually, calm was restored, players hugged and high-fived, and the spirit of the contest was brought to the forefront. The Moontowers and the Playboys had tied! And that is how it would be remembered for all time or at least for another hour because by then, it was uncertain whether my players had even known they had been in a game.

Game 2

It seemed innocent enough, our players lounging in lawn chairs or on benches underneath tents. Someone cooked up some chicken, and we enjoyed that while having a couple of beers. Then someone pulled out a tequila bottle. Then a shipment of Fireball arrived in what I thought was a bucket of baseballs. Soon, the entire team gathered underneath a shade tree, and things unraveled. Suffice it to say, I am not sure any of us knew there was to be a second game. It is a wonder we took the field at all. But take the field we did, and what a game it turned out to be.

Between games, Bryan Hood, the Yardbirds' coach, and I had decided we would determine the home team by holding a race. It would be someone in a hot dog costume versus someone in a peanut outfit. Our choice to run was Will "Wheels" Bryant, the fastest player on our team and maybe the fastest guy in the league. I am unsure if Fireball was involved, but the Peanut crossed home plate a few feet ahead of the Hot Dog. Thankfully the Peanut was the costume Wheels was wearing, and we earned home team honors.

It was agreed beforehand that each team would again call the pitches for their squad from behind the mound. Caruthers had enough of umpiring after the first game and spent much of the time between games scolding me for putting him in that position. He declared he would never ump again. With no viable alternatives, I was designated as our team's signal caller and thought I called a pretty solid, albeit uneven game. The only time I even engaged with a player on either team was when a shot hit off the left-field net and fell back onto the field. The outfielder fielded the ball and held the runner to a single. When the play was over I didn't think much about it and waited as the ball was thrown back to the pitcher. And then I noticed something from the corner of my eye. It was Del Conte. He was calling time out and advancing toward me from his third-base coaching box.

"Say, uh, Blue, I thought if the ball hit off the net like that, it would be a ground-rule double?" It was more a declaration rather than a statement.

"No, the net is like a fence. The ball is still in play."

"You sure about that?"

"Yes." After that, he looked at me for a second, then scratched his chin.

"Well, I don't like it." He then paused for moment while staring at me with ire and added, "No, I don't like that at all." He then slowly turned and walked away.

The Yardbirds got out to a five-run lead but slowed down from there, and the game turned into the survival of the fittest as Jake was throwing harder than I had seen him all year. He had gone to a rival high school in Round Rock, and I could see he wanted nothing more than to beat his former rivals. Even though the Yardbirds opened up a lead, we weren't finished. The House finally showed his baseball prowess and smashed one into orbit over the left-field foul pole. Later I heard the crack of the bat and looked up to see another ball disappearing over the left-field fence. I turned to see who hit it, and Bennie Blades was rounding the bases before me. Ben was going through a divorce, and I could tell that lately his mind seemed to be on other things, so I knew it was a special moment for him as his sons were there to see it. He needed a shot of encouragement, and this was it. He returned to the dugout, bewildered as if he didn't understand what had happened. For the most part, he probably didn't, as I found him sitting on Johnny D's lap just a few minutes later, sharing shots of Fireball. But the cries of laughter and backslaps went on for several innings as the home run tied the game and gave us the lead.

Finally, late in the game, Wheels was on second base when he got caught up in what is affectionately known as a "pickle" or "hotbox." He started toward third and then reversed course, and back and forth he went. For whatever reason, perhaps due to his speed or the other team's increasing blood alcohol content, the pickle went on for at least seven throws which is unheard of. Eventually, with the peanut costume now discarded, he made a break for home and roared around third and flew to the plate. The throw came in, and Wheels arrived in a cloud of dust. Despite there being no sanctioned umpire to make the call, there was no doubt he slid under the tag, and we had an insurance run to put us up by two.

We won the game by a run, and afterward came hugs and laughter and all the blessings that go along with a hard-earned sandlot victory preceded by several hours of drinking and a hot dog–peanut race. Afterward, in the post-game dugout meeting, I awarded the game ball to Bennie Blades. Later my wife informed me I should've given it to Wheels, and I could see her point, and some may doubt my decision, including myself. But as I see it, the younger players are still in their prime. Athletic endeavors such as those they accomplish are not inconsistent with their abilities. For the old-timers, we are one wrong step away from a career-ending episode. Hitting a home run well into your fifties could be the final moment of glory for many of us. We just never know. Either way, the celebration continued until the light began to fade. And as the dust was still floating in the air, I could hear the shouts from across the parking lot as players and their families drifted toward their cars, each guy excitedly recounting his role that afternoon to his family. It was a moment I hoped would live on forever and that nothing would ever change.

CHAPTER 22
FOREVER FAMILY

Baseball is not a sport you can achieve individually.
— Curt Schilling

My mom died on October 26, 2022, just two days after the doubleheader with the Playboys and the Yardbirds. The glow from that triumphant Sunday afternoon at the Long Time was shattered in less than forty-eight hours. That day had been one of the greatest of my life—this one arguably the worst.

Death had been not far away the last few months. Two uncles died in the summer, and by the end of the year, an aunt passed well. It was actually while in San Antonio at one of my uncle's funerals, when my brother Mark and I received a call from a hospital in Austin that my mother had what doctors thought was a stroke. She was diagnosed with dementia several years previously, and I often received calls from various hospitals that she had fallen or perhaps was having a minor stroke. Mark lives in Colorado, so the bulk of daily care for my mom revolved around me, but he and I consulted each other on every decision. This situation was nothing we hadn't encountered before. Dementia, like Alzheimer's, is a dreadful disease, and we don't have a firm grasp on what causes it or how it will manifest in each person. In my mother's case, we noticed her decline a few years before when she got lost while driving or fell and injured herself. One fall resulted in a severe cut to her face, so we decided it was no longer safe for her to live alone.

For several years following my father's death in 1988, Mom lived in various houses in Northwest Austin and persevered with the same toughness and resilience she taught my brother and me. She had several suitors, boyfriends, partners, whatever they may be called, who danced with her in the town's senior centers and dance halls. But in recent years, she spent more time alone until it became unsafe for her to continue to do so. Unfortunately, dementia offers no road map for the family, so my brother and I based our decisions on the information we had at the time. Sometimes we made the right call and looking back, sometimes made the wrong one. Either way, we did the best we could.

Eventually, we decided Mom should live in an environment with structure and more access to friends, so we moved her into an independent retirement facility, where she lived for years. Ultimately, we realized she'd be better off in assisted living and finally in memory care when it became clear her condition had worsened. She had been living in the memory care unit for just a few months when the call came about what was at first thought to be a serious stroke. We knew a call like this would be an eventuality, yet it was still a jolt when the news came. It was as if I spent years in a freefall and finally hit the ground.

The hospital ran a battery of tests, and it turned out not to be a stroke but rather a bacteria that had entered her body. She was in septic shock. By the time I reached the hospital, she was almost in a coma. She could recognize me but couldn't talk. I visited with her every day for the next few days while my brother kept tabs on her from Colorado. Her condition didn't improve, and it was decided to place her in hospice. From that point, we let nature take its course.

My mom, like most mothers, was caring and nurturing and lived a life of meaning and purpose. She was the foundation not only of my life but, in a strange twist of occurrences, was part of the reason the Moontowers were even in existence. My family moved to Austin in 1969, and she joined several bridge groups while my father continued his role as a draftsman in the military. Playing bridge is what people of her generation did. It was their social activity. And in one of these groups, she met a woman named Joyce Hartenstein. Joyce had a son named Chris, who was in my brother's first-grade class and has remained a friend to us. At that time, she also began working in the front office at Reagan High School as a data processing coordinator and became friends with a teacher named Jo Hill. Jo had a daughter named Julia, who was also in the class with my brother and Chris, and they were friends. Julia had a brother named Elliott. And so, the very seeds of my little group of friends were planted as far back as that time.

Most interesting is that my mother remained close to those people for the rest of her life. And I followed suit. Elliott and I have known each other for over fifty years. Surrounding herself with great people is a gift she gave to me. From the time I was young, I knew I had people who were warm and engaging and who gave me a life of comfort and joy from which I could pursue the dreams I had as a youngster. And along for the ride came the rest of my friends who make up a bulk of the Moontowers contingent: Johnny D, Malcom, Spark, Turner, Elliott, and Vanek. Slugger McGoo and his wife Kerri, as well as her brother David. These people were important to me when I was ten and are important now. They are part of my family. That's a testament to the parents I had and the rest of us as well. We grew up around tenets that encourage family, whether it was the people in your home, the ones you grew up with, or the ones you meet today. It's about being part of something larger than yourself.

Within those parameters, I see my new family, the Moontowers, shaping up. They have an unselfishness, a resolve to make the whole better than the parts. I sense this by how we interact not only at our games but when we meet each other's families or when something needs to be done that helps out the group. It isn't always perfect, but it's a natural outgrowth of what was instilled in us by our parents and the people they kept around as friends.

Watching someone die was foreign to me. I had seen unspeakable tragedy up close at the earthquake and 9/11, but despite the pain I held within, those incidents seemed distant, as if I was an outsider who didn't belong. My father's death was over almost before it began, so watching someone pass in real time was new and I wasn't sure how to deal with it. As I visited Mom in her final days, I read literature on how to deal with the dying. The overarching message I learned was to attempt to make someone as comfortable as possible. I sat with her in the afternoons when I visited and read Bible verses to her, hoping to ease her pain. I put on her favorite music and tried to make her aware of my presence.

On the day she died, I was working in my office at my house. It was late afternoon when her caregiver called and said I should come and be with her. By then, she was out of the hospital and spending her final days more comfortably in her own home. When they told me the end was growing near, I did my best to face it. I went to my room, changed my clothes into something nice, and combed my hair. I don't know why. I just remember that I did. And then I drove up to where she was and called my wife and my son Alex and told them to come to say goodbye. I arrived first and sat with her, and soon Liz arrived. Then Alex. He went straight to her, sat down, and told her how much she meant to him and that he loved her and always would. It was truly a moment of grace, a son carrying forward the feelings of his father with courage and strength. I only hope that people can hear such beautiful words in the final moments of their lives.

When the end came, she was listening to Andy Williams, one of her favorite singers. Her breathing became labored, and I could see she was starting to go. But then, suddenly, a spark came to her eye. Alex noticed it first. She seemed to awaken and smile. She looked directly at us, right into our eyes. Her eyes were alert and strong, and Alex exclaimed, "Hi, Granny! It's me, Alex." And I said the same, "Hi, Mom. We're here." I just kept saying hi repeatedly, hoping she'd recognize us. Liz smiled at her and told her she was there for her too. And for a few seconds, she was with us, together in the room. But, like the final flicker of a candle before it goes out, the moment of clarity was gone. A couple of minutes later, she passed. She simply stopped breathing, and it was over. It was now early in the evening, and I remember thinking that was the first moment I had ever been alive that my mother wasn't alive too.

SHINE THE LIGHT

We got home later, and I sat on the couch, trying to sort out my feelings. Soon the condolences rolled in, most by text, but there were a couple of calls. And then the doorbell rang. It was Elliott and his wife, Gina. They came inside, and I grabbed onto him and cried. He had recently gone through the same thing with his mother, Jo. He had even told me how the final days would play out, and that is exactly what happened. And now it was comforting to have someone else with me who intimately knew the travesty that was dementia. And soon, the words of encouragement trickled in from the team. Even though I had only known them for a few months, they were part of my family now. The one my mother started so long ago.

A few days later, at her funeral, I said thank you to her for the life she had lived. The sentiment was for her but was meant for all the mothers *and* fathers who had touched so many. Both my parents led rich lives, full of decent people, role models who helped contour our paths before we even knew them. And as with my father's death, the weeks following my mother's funeral were filled with reflection as I tried to piece together how life would endure. I wasn't sure which was worse, suffering the instantaneous gut punch of my father's death and the resulting self-flagellation it brought. Or watching the light slowly fade from my mother until there was nothing left but her voice. And then, one day, that too was gone.

We buried her alongside my father at a military cemetery in San Antonio. All our extended family was there, many the same as had been at my father's funeral nearly three decades before. Among them were the same cousins I played baseball with in the early seventies and with whom I shared the same values that originated with our grandparents in Mexico two centuries ago.

And with her passing, death consumed me in November and December of 2021. I can't say it was constantly on my mind, but I cried during TV commercials or driving around on the simplest of errands. A new family in the Moontowers became essential as I was now an orphan with my only brother far away in Colorado. I had old faces to rely on but new faces to encourage me. Faces to stretch me and challenge me and make me grow again, as my parents had done when I was a boy. In a way, I've been seeking people to admire since my father died when I was twenty-two, searching for his approval in the ones with whom I spend most of my time. He couldn't see my brother or me grow up into what we would become or spend meaningful time with his grandsons, which troubled me for many years. But my mother was allowed that opportunity, and for that, I was grateful despite how painful the end would be.

Now that neither of my parents would ever watch me play again, I thought about how I had been when they were in the stands. I remember searching for them, sitting among the other parents before every game, just to ensure they were there. I hope I can live up to what they wanted for me while watching all those hours in the sweltering heat. The memory of them brings me back to when I was young, back to the goodness of summer afternoons when my friends and I played until dark and then talked about the big leagues late into the night, hoping that someday it would be us under the bright lights. And when I close my eyes, it can be 1975 all over again when dreams were more real than they seem today. When, in my deepest slumber, the crack of the bat opened up the light in my heart, and I saw the trees in my yard, and the ball rose above them and continued to soar as far as I wanted it to go.

SHINE THE LIGHT

And soon, life returned to normal, and we were back on the field, playing as we had before. The Moontowers are a new family for me, created through the same principles my parents had taught me: effort and resilience. Baseball is a game born of routine, and though I had a heavy heart, I understood everyone has something they carry around inside, some privately held anguish. Everyone suffers. Everyone grieves. And everyone moves forward. One pitch at a time. One out at a time. One base at a time. And I was thankful I had a new family to carry me, in the same spirit as the one I had before.

CHAPTER 23

MEANING AND PURPOSE

I think about baseball when I wake up in the morning. I think about it all day and I dream about it at night. The only time I don't think about it is when I'm playing it.

—Carl Yastrzemski

As the days shortened and brought a certain crispness to the autumn air, our season came down to its final embers. We played a couple of games at Govalle, which is nothing like the Long Time, but is symbolic of what sandlot baseball should be. There are a few weeds in the outfield and bare spots where dirt has crept up on what was probably once a nice grass infield. On this particular Sunday afternoon, we played a team called the Grackles, and sure enough, with some of our pitchers gone or injured, the game got out of hand.

Marshall Newhouse had been asking me if he could pitch. The nephew of former Dallas Cowboys running back Robert Newhouse, Marshall grew up playing "select" baseball in the Dallas area. Select is a league for players with advanced skills, so I figured he would be fine on the mound. During warm-up, his rhythm was easy, and he had good velocity. Unfortunately, when the first batter stepped into the box, he couldn't find the plate. After eight batters had reached base with no outs, I had to go and get him, and when I went to the mound, he told me, "Coach, my heart is beating really fast." He played ten years in the NFL, but sandlot baseball made him nervous all over again. It was probably like when he first took the mound in Little League, and I felt for him.

The pitching fiasco resulted in me searching for anyone who could essentially grip the ball to take the mound. Eventually, Elliott came over and said he could pitch to which I immediately said no. Even in my panic it was a hard no. It wasn't so much that I wouldn't let him; it was simply that I had known him for half a century, and never once had I seen him pitch or even offer. Elliott and I rarely disagree, although we've had spirited debates about the merits of his beloved TCU Horned Frogs and my Texas Longhorns. But, as the deficit reached double digits, I grew desperate and said if he could prove he could throw, I would put him in. We eventually went to the bullpen mound behind the dugout, and I got down like the catcher. He wound up and threw the ball a few times. One ball after another hit the mitt each time with a defensible speed, and so like that, a pitcher was born.

I said, "Okay, maybe you can pitch," and I put him on the mound. And he wasn't bad; he was downright good. He has a natural delivery, and his follow-through resembles that of one of the greatest pitchers, a fellow named Bob Gibson. During two innings, Elliott struck out four hitters. He also balked once or twice. But the bottom line was, who really cares? He pushed himself out of his comfort zone for his friends, just as Marshall had done. And that is all anyone can reasonably ask.

We played the Yardbirds again. This game was also on a Sunday, just one day after the University of Texas football team had suffered a crushing defeat at the hands of Kansas. All of us were certain Del Conte would not be there. But, sure enough, just before game time, his car pulled up, and out he came. He never said anything, but deep down, I think he needed the show of brotherhood to help regain some sense of normalcy. It isn't normal to lose to Kansas on the football field, and as the athletic director, he is ultimately responsible for the well-being of the sports teams. He seemed a little gloomy and wasn't his usual umpire-baiting self, but he was there and eager to cheer on anyone who might come his way at third base.

Before each game, we did a team cheer, usually something like "Moontowers! On three . . . one . . . two . . . three . . . Moontowers!" This time, Elliott called in Del Conte and asked if he wanted to come up with the cheer, where he said, "Yeah, DON'T LOSE TO KANSAS, ON THREE!" And so that's the phrase that led the Moontowers that day onto the field— "DON'T LOSE TO KANSAS!" Naturally, we lost.

We had a lot of supporters and players drinking beer afterward. And though the shadows began to creep in, it felt good that we played baseball in the half-light of the deepening fall afternoon. It was as close as I had ever been to playing in the cool autumn air of a World Series. And as we packed to leave, an assortment of goodbyes and the usual "Let's get together" ensued as the players drifted toward their cars in the rutted parking lot. I didn't know what would happen to our team in the offseason. I believed we were onto something special, but you never know how things will play out between the end of one season and the start of the next.

However, I knew I was eager to get back on the field with this group, as my passion for baseball had been slowly, then suddenly, renewed. The feeling wasn't as it had been when I was in San Luis Obispo, and I couldn't wait to get out of the dugout. Back then, the passion for the game was lost. What I had enjoyed so much growing up didn't hold the same importance as an adult.

I had even spoken to Selber about it while contemplating what I felt. He has been so busy as a professor we rarely spoke anymore, just an assortment of emails to replay certain events from our childhood, almost to see if we still remembered them the same. It was unique that we discussed our loss of baseball more cohesively, each of us accepting what had become an eventuality, that the game was no longer part of our daily ritual. Every morning since we were kids, he studied the box scores of each major league game from the previous day. He kept his own statistics and, for decades, kept a running tally of each player's batting average. But, like me, he said he moved on from the sport and was now more interested in soccer.

Spark says he rarely watches a game on TV, preferring the NBA to MLB. I guess as the body changes, so does the mind. The feelings you have reflect where you are in life. Things gain or lose importance, and baseball lost importance. It had been banished to the attic, where things were stored and eventually forgotten.

But what began with my interest in Joe Maddon and then getting back on the field around such inspiring people, the dying ashes started to burn again. When something once enjoyed comes back in a new context, it can be rediscovered. You can examine it for what it means today rather than what it once held. And so, one day following that final game, while holding a baseball,

I looked at it closely. I turned it repeatedly in my hand, rotating it back and forth ever so slowly. The seams are sewn together, and there is no beginning or end. They just loop back to where they started, stitching together two things that become one, two halves that make a whole. And that is how I saw baseball again. The game led me back to where I started—summers past combined with summers present.

And it wasn't just about Elliott or me. Many times in the past few months, I saw the same smiles I had seen when I was an eight-year-old and watched a teammate get his first hit, catch his first fly ball or strike out his first hitter. Today I see the faces of the wives and the children proud of their fathers, not necessarily for any great play they might have made, but for being out there, competing. And I see how the game is changing the ones who play it. Scott Malcom wasn't an outstanding athlete when he was younger and even for us was more of a base coach than a player. But in one game, he pulled me aside and very politely asked if he could bat. I recognized it had taken him courage to even consider the idea. The prospect of failure loomed yet he still found it within himself to give it a go. So I sent him up there. He struck out but had a couple of good swings. When he came back to the bench, he thanked me. He wanted to prove to himself that he could do it. And even though he struck out, he had been at the plate with a bat in his hand, where anything was possible again.

Later on, I thought about Casey Dunn. He is a professional photographer who came to us through one of our younger players after the season had started. He ordinarily didn't say much and recently had a baby, so he missed a couple of games, and I didn't get to know him that well. One day, though, while caring for his newborn, his wife gave him one hour to stretch his legs. And where did he go? He came to a game and wound up hitting a home run! I wondered if he might one day tell his child about that home run—how he hit it on a one-hour break and how he sprinted around the bases to make it home just in time.

And there, alongside me, was baseball again, seen from the other side—not determination and grit but smiles and joy when anyone, men and women, joins each other in play and a sense of oneness. It was just like the summer days of my youth when the game grabbed ahold of me. It dawned on me that it had never let go.

Maybe my entire life had pointed to spreading the game rather than shrinking from and internalizing it. So much of growing up was an inward struggle, coming through the cracks and reaching, striving for the light. But with a new perspective, I could show baseball's beauty to others and share its secrets instead of hoarding them for myself, taking the bright light I had been reaching for and letting it shine on others. I realized the hold baseball had on me my entire life, and I was wrong to think I needed to leave it behind. Carl Jung said, "The afternoon of life is just as full of meaning as the morning; only its meaning and purpose are different." I agree, for baseball, even when I thought it was no longer relevant, revealed itself to me in a more profound way.

And now, the season was over. Some of us were still in one piece. Most had suffered some injury or another. But to a player, we had walked through another door and into a new period in our lives. I knew this to be true because it was what I felt. The memories of baseball that faded with youth were now emblazoned on our minds and hearts. We were on a team, and the game was as real today as it was then, even more so. And with a hint of sagacity that comes with age, it is easier to understand, in real time, what was happening. How friendships were being forged. How memories were being made. How sandlot baseball created community, made people smile, and eased our daily drama; for three hours on any weekend afternoon, it could send us back to a time when life seemed easy. It's part of learning, which hopefully never ends, like the baseball games in my childhood dreams. And I was thankful I had let the game reenter my life. Baseball returned to me. And I was better for that.

Unfortunately, heath-wise, I was not better. The end of the season for me meant something else entirely. I had surgery on November 15. It was just a torn meniscus, and I was hobbling around by the end of the day and walking a day later, but it still meant I had a couple of months of rehab in front of me. I had to. I had a season to get ready for. Meanwhile, life continued to happen. CDC let the Moontowers sit in his suite during a Texas game. Paul Hedrick, the CEO of Tecovas, gave us discounts at his store for Christmas. Ben O'Meara did the same for Huckberry, the company where he worked. This was more than a collection of baseball players; it was a little family. We didn't have text messaging when we were kids, so the ability to keep up with one another through text kept the group together. When someone needed something, they could rely on one of us.

One day, someone needed help doing an odd job, and he called on the team for some assistance. Another guy needed help getting a car after he had wrecked his, and two days later, he was sitting in a new model. And finally, my son Alex passed the Texas Bar Exam. He graduated from law school a year before and had failed the bar twice. On his third try, he passed. As I told him then, what anyone will remember is that he kept going. No one reflects on the story of someone who passes on the first try; they remember who refused to quit. He has always hustled, both scholastically and while backing up first base from the catcher position—something very few continue to do. I told him that fortitude he showed behind the plate would be rewarded in his professional life, and it would be a teaching moment he could relay to his own children somewhere in the future.

Speaking of Christmas, the Moontowers celebrated the holiday spirit with an end-of-the-year party. Almost everyone on the team showed up at Koko's Bavarian Beer Garden on the east side of town. Charles Attal is one of the owners and graciously gave us the run of the place for the night. He couldn't play as often as he liked but was always willing to help with our off-field needs, proving that a Moontower could contribute in more ways than one. We gave out silly awards like the Long Drive, which went to Waco. He won this because he drove down from Waco to every practice, game, and team function. He was awarded a nine-dollar used driver found in a discount bin at a second-hand sporting goods store. The best cheerleader award went to Duddy, who received a set of pom-poms. Duddy's band, Midland, eventually played a concert in Austin at the ACL-Live Moody Theater right before Christmas. (Every venue in Austin is called Moody.) At one point, he yelled out, "Are there any Moontowers in the house?" It was the best present any of us could've received.

The pickle award went to Wheels. We gave him jars of pickles *and* peanuts (for winning the race in his costume). Marshall and Legs got the GQ award for turning their uniform pants into cut-off shorts. And, of course, the Pearle Vision Award went to Del Conte. He received a pair of reading glasses to give to an ump next year as part of his schtick. And we finally got our baseball cards. They resembled the bubble gum cards Selber and I collected in the flea market when we were kids. After the party, the team went to a country music dance hall called Donn's Depot to finish the night. I rode there with Marshall, both of us pressed into the cab of his 1972 Chevy C-10, listening to Billy Strings deafeningly loud. Of course, two days later, half the team wound up testing positive for COVID.

CHAPTER 24

SANDLOT REVOLUTION

Every strike brings me closer to the next home run.

—Babe Ruth

And so, after fifty-five years on this earth, my life had finally caught up with itself; I was starting over again. Two thousand twenty-two brought a new year and a new season. And like when the first warm spring night ushers in the sense of renewal, I felt energized and ready to embark on whatever the journey would bring. The Moontowers were back in business, with a whirlwind of activity to greet us at a new starting line.

In January, Elliott and I were offered the chance to appear on the *Sandlot Revolution* podcast. Our friends Northcutt, Bryan Hood, and Howard are trying to turn sandlot baseball into a national phenomenon. They want to build it into something resembling Little League baseball but with the sandlot texture and feel. Hopefully, cities around the country will create their own sandlot leagues, and teams will travel to other towns for games and form a national syndicate. We were only glad to tell the story of how we started and hoped that it would inspire anyone listening to do the same where they lived.

We added new players to the team. Gregg Donnelly, or Triple G, became a new outfielder. He's been a fixture at every game since the team's inception and learned of his invitation by opening a Christmas present from Elliott. He had dated Elliott's daughter, Peyton, for years but had to go through the approval process like everyone else. That process consists of Elliott and I discussing the merits of each player and how they will fit in with the team. The dynamic we have right now is as close to perfect as possible, so we are reticent to create disruptions. Still, we need pitching. Jake's arm is on its last legs. I could tell it was hurting, and at the start of the new year, he was laboring to throw as had been the case late last season. So, we added Bob Mott. Bob is from San Luis Obispo, which is interesting because, for a brief period in the mid-nineties, my son Alex, Bob, Chris Del Conte, and I had all lived, unbeknownst to each other, in San Luis simultaneously. And now, we are on the same baseball team nearly thirty years later.

I started moving around reasonably well, and by early February found myself at a nearby school, throwing a tennis ball against the wall, just like when I was a kid. There I was, doing it again, trying to strengthen my arm for the upcoming season. The leg was heading toward becoming functional again, but I still had a limp to my gait and was not running by the time we took the field for the first time in the new year. We had a scrimmage in nearby Dripping Springs against our favorite opponents, the Yardbirds. It was a cold January day, and I was looking forward to returning to the Long Time when the sun shined and the tequila and Fireball flowed. But until then, we still had to get the gears moving.

It was fun to see the guys. The grass was dead and the sky a dull winter gray with more than a hint of a chill in the air. But when I heard the distinctive sound of the ball hitting the mitt, I remembered why we came out here to work on our rediscovered craft. It sounded like it had when I worked out with my teammates in the dead of winter back in high school, trying to get a little better each day.

Elliott and I also began a relationship with a non-profit organization called RBI Austin. Each of us purchased a table at their fundraising gala and met with the director to see where we could fit in. RBI works with underserved children and, through baseball, helps pilot them through the pitfalls of life. The local chapter began at Reagan High School, where the two of us had attended many years ago. Being around underserved children was not foreign to us. Growing up in Northeast Austin, our neighborhoods were solidly middle class. Still, some surrounding areas that fed into the school were decidedly on the lower end of the financial spectrum. Although none of my close friends were affected by severe economic issues, I could tell that many of my classmates came from households that most likely did not resemble mine. And it is an honor that we could do whatever might help someone avoid the indignities that come with being in that station in life.

Finally, the biggest accolade that could come to us occurred when Jack Sanders called and offered to make the Moontowers the Opening Day opponent for his Texas Playboys. It was a lot to take in. In less than one year, we had gone from two guys wanting to play baseball again to the guest of honor at the home of the most storied sandlot team in the country. It was a testament to the players who made up our team and our fans who came out in droves to support us and the entire movement. We were highly honored, so I organized a pair of extra practices and scrimmages to help us prepare. And now, with Opening Day approaching, I was excited as my health was getting closer to being good to go.

I went to bed the night before the game with dreams of homering in the first at-bat and rounding the bases victoriously, perhaps pulling a double clutch at second base like Kirk Gibson of the Dodgers in the 1988 World Series. Everything was aligning perfectly. The Moontowers. The Playboys. My return to the game and maybe even another home run to bookend this fabulously heroic tale. Hey, one can dream, can't they?

I wish, on that cloudless day in March when I stepped to the plate as the leadoff hitter to start the season against the Playboys, that I sent that first pitch far beyond the outfield wall at the Long Time. And I wish I rounded the bases knowing that my career was now completely over, having homered once again in my final at-bat. And I wish I returned to the dugout and took off my cleats, announcing for all time that I was done. But it didn't happen that way, not even close. What happened instead was better.

A storm had blown in the night before, and the morning dawned with freezing temperatures. But by the time I got to the Long Time, the sun was shining and the sky was a brilliant blue, like the new young spring. The field was alert with people arriving, saying hello, talking to one another, and enjoying a communal moment while they took in a sandlot baseball game.

When I stepped to the plate as the leadoff hitter in the game, I hoped for a waist-high fastball like the one I had taken out of the park in San Luis Obispo in the nineties. Instead, a knuckle curve broke away from me and caught the outside part of the plate for a strike. The next pitch was the same, and in my attempt to smite it, I missed by two feet, leaving me behind in the count 0–2. I even muttered under my breath to Howard, the Playboys' catcher and my first true friend in sandlot, "Geez, Howard. Can you not throw me a fastball and let me take my cut?"

He might've laughed, I don't remember, but as the moment grew dark, everything suddenly turned my way. The next four pitches came nowhere near the plate, so I walked just as I had in my first at-bat in the over-fifty league and in my first at-bat as a Moontower. That was my job. I'm the leadoff hitter. I'm supposed to get on base, and so I did. The next pitch got past Howard, and I beat the throw to second, but my running ability had reached its limit on the journey to the base. So, I called timeout and asked for a pinch-runner. And when I came back to the dugout, I settled into a nice spot on the bench and surveyed the scene around me. I looked around and thought about what would've happened had I called it quits back in San Luis Obispo when I went out seemingly on top. I looked around again and thought about what I would've missed out on, what I would've never seen.

Before the game, instead of playing the national anthem, we all gathered and listened to one of the local Austin bands play the Woody Guthrie song, "This Land Is Your Land." Hundreds of people lined both fences and were backed up behind home plate. And I saw the entire crowd singing—men, women, families, children in strollers, fans of both teams. There were beanies and cowboy hats, lumberjack shirts, and sandals. No one was on their phones. And I saw Elliott singing, the kid I grew up with who had traveled the world looking for a community. The kid who wanted to keep the old man out. And when I saw our teammates singing, the twenty-three-year-olds alongside the guys pushing sixty, I knew he had succeeded on both accounts. Although the old man may have settled into our joints, ligaments, and bones, he was not in our minds, hearts, or souls.

And then it happened. I heard the crack of the bat. It was that particular sound when you know a ball is taking flight, and I looked up. The last thing I remember seeing is the white baseball climbing through the endless blue sky, higher and higher, above the net in left, higher even until it dropped behind the trees beyond the left field fence. And I looked up to see who had hit it. It was Slugger McGoo. Greg Morisey. Modesta Sander. Ol' G-Moe. Fifty-eight-years old. The guy who said he only wanted to be a coach. The guy who slipped into the batting cage when I wasn't looking. And the guy who ducked out of the lineup when I wasn't looking as well.

And as he rounded third and made his way to the plate he put his head down. He touched home amid the backslapping and hugs that usually accompany a momentus occasion such as home run and made a beeline to an area behind the dugout. I watched him as I sat down on the bench, and at that moment finally realized why I had returned to baseball. It was because I needed baseball, just as I had when I was young.

But this time around, I needed it differently. This time was about sharing it with others. Sharing it with my sons and watching my friends share it with their kids. Instead of me trying to make the All-Stars, impress a coach, or win a championship, it was now the shared experience of being among my pals, laughing and watching as we grew together. It was about welcoming the new faces of Austin as they contributed to a time in our city when people joined together, sang, and played an old-fashioned game on a sandlot. A time when they cheered and jeered and laughed and cried, but most of all, a time when they took in the moment together.

The former MLB Commissioner, A. Bartlett Giamatti, once said that baseball is meant to break your heart. I believe that is true, but I also believe it's meant to mend it back together. And as I looked back over my years in the game, I recalled the many times I lost. So many times when I didn't win. So often, when I was on the outside looking in. Yet through all that, baseball helped make me who I am and, even more importantly, showed me who I am not. It gave me a family besides my flesh and blood, and it gave me people who shared this crazy ride called life. From when I was a bat boy for my brother's team to teaching the game to my sons and now playing in my older age, baseball created that atmosphere, that stage, that backdrop in which I moved from childhood into adulthood. I am but a reflection of all the people I interacted with, the people I played against, and those who cherished and loved the same game I did. Win or lose, baseball made the whole thing worth doing. And as the Moontower mission statement says:

We believe in baseball.

We believe in what it teaches us while we are here.

We believe in keeping it alive for those who come after us.

And I looked over at Slugger McGoo, standing quietly by himself behind the dugout. He was looking down, so I called over to him. He paused but then looked back at me just as the glint of the afternoon sunlight caught his eye. And I saw, in that moment, that he had been crying.

SWEATPANTS

Every day is a new opportunity. You can build on yesterday's success or put its failures behind and start over again. That's the way life is, with a new game every day, and that's the way baseball is.

—Bob Feller

More than four hundred people attended the Moontower-Playboy game. It was a classic back-and-forth affair and didn't end until our pitcher, Chris Ellis, struck out the final batter with the tying and winning runs on base. We ran onto the field and jumped on him as if we had won the World Series. And in a way, we had, as with that win I felt we were fully a part of the sandlot family. I was excited not only about our success but about what lay ahead for us in our second year as we continue to evolve. Elliott has continued to pitch, striking out an additional three batters in his only mound appearance this season. I discovered the knee wasn't my only leg issue. My hip had also hurt the entire season, so I had it checked. The result is degenerative arthritis, something my grandfather in North Carolina suffered from and, for me, would one day require a hip replacement.

As for the rest of the team, we've added a few new faces to the mix but are still primarily made up of the original cast of characters. Zach Suarez and Mike DiAlfonso joined as pitchers. Both of those guys were in perfect shape. We called them Rico Suave and Magic Mike. Neither is old enough even to know what we mean. In addition, we've had two babies born. One player got married, while two more got engaged. Bob Mott broke the pitching machine again, only the second time ever. Mark Turner, who had never played organized baseball, got a base hit for which he received the game ball. He had grown up a European soccer player and a tremendous skier in the Alps, yet being awarded that dirty brown ball may have been his finest sports achievement. He could not stop grinning from ear to ear and talked about it for days.

The first Moontower to quit was Brian Vanek, who declared he was moving to Fort Collins, Colorado. He said he couldn't resist because there was so much open space with free and available parking as far as the eye could see. There must be a cosmic connection to Colorado because Thomas Tyng and I spent some time together near Vail in the winter, throwing a baseball in the snow, trying to stay sharp. And my older son, Andrew, came down from Denver and joined his brother Alex and me in a Moontowers game, the first time we were all on a field together in a team competition! He said he couldn't tell if it was real or something from a dream.

The Moontowers also officially partnered with RBI Austin, which is an important outreach we wholeheartedly support. In the summer of 2022, we held our first fundraiser for the organization by showing the movie, *The Sandlot*. It was Elliott's idea and required us to call on the unique talents of several of our teammates to pull it off. We rented the State Theatre in downtown Austin and hosted invitees from the public as well as the sandlot community for an auction and the movie. Our designers created movie posters and came up with themed drinks to accent the attendees' evening. Ultimately, we raised over $12,000 for RBI to help build a home complex for their kids, complete with their own baseball field. We will continue to raise money for them and hope the new field will someday be our home. In the meantime, we continue to play at the Long Time, Govalle, and wherever else we can find a game.

Oh—and I finally got to play for the University of Texas . . . sort of. Chris Del Conte was generous enough to let us play a game at Disch-Falk Field, where I tried out for the Longhorns many years before. It was a Sunday night during the summer, and Del Conte opened the field for us for a game between the Moontowers and a combination of the Yardbirds and Playboys. Our goal was to thank the people who had helped us form the team and get involved in the league.

Before the game, current Texas head coach David Pierce gave all the players a tour of the facilities, including the stadium's batting cages and locker rooms. The place was magnificent, and Pierce even threw some BP to both teams as we got ready for the game. It was an extraordinary experience and one which anyone who was there will no doubt ever forget.

Following in the long line of legendary Texas coaches, from Cliff Gustafson through Augie Garrido, Pierce has been outstanding in his own right, having led Texas to the College World Series three times in his first six seasons at the helm. During the game, though, I was playing second base when a ground ball came my way. With my impending hip issue, I hobbled over to field it, and by the time I threw it to first base the runner was safe. When I got back to the dugout, Pierce was standing there, and he immediately got in my face and proclaimed that my footwork wasn't good enough and that I needed to work on it. I tried to tell him I was fifty-six years old and needed a hip replacement, to which he replied, "Oh, that's a bunch of bull!" It was so great. I was getting chewed out by the Longhorns' head coach. I couldn't help but laugh but took the advice to heart, and in the next inning, when another grounder came my way, I got over there a little quicker to field it and threw the runner out. I could hear him from the dugout yelling, "See, that's a lot better!" So, in a weird way, I felt like nearly forty years later, I had finally made it to the Longhorns, with the head coach watching over me, helping me become a better player and not putting up with any of my lip.

The journey from idea to playing a game in front of nearly five hundred people at the most storied field in the country was what I hoped to capture here. But how we got from there to here is nothing short of remarkable and calls into the power of a focused and talented group, led by our design team of Ryan Caruthers, Will Bryant, and Sean Curran. Our marketing department of Sean, Ben O'Meara, and Carter Blackwell. With our team moms, Liz Matthews, Kerri Monroe, and Gina Hill, and with our loyal, ever-growing fan base, the Austin Moontowers hope to be part of the Austin sandlot baseball scene for years to come. We hope the team and the sandlot league grow and thrive and remain part of the landscape that defines this ever-changing hometown for so many of us.

And if there is one thing I will take from this time in my life, it's seeing the authentic and deep-set smiles on the faces of the players and our fans. Our team photographer, Carter Blackwell, shoots photographs of most of our games and continually captures these moments for us. When I see his photos, they blend with the ones of my youth that emerge from my mind and, most likely, my soul. I see again, not as something distant, but images enriched with the sounds and smells of today, which bring those memories to life. It is remarkable when people, some of whom are moving into the autumn of their lives, join others still in their springtime to create a place for baseball fans of all ages to enjoy. I take that feeling home every time we play, a profound joy emanating from someplace deep within.

Growing up, I never fished or hunted like so many kids in Texas. I played baseball. It was what was presented in front of me, and so I peered into it, found its crevices, and explored them, seeking to find something about the game, its people, its places, and how they fit into my life. And after this year as the coach and player, father and teammate, again, I realized it wasn't childish to love baseball the way I did, and it's okay to reconnect with childhood, even if you have to grow up. And I was thankful for never completely walking away from it.

Life gives you moments, but you can't always realize them for what they are until they've passed by. But I knew instantly when I first saw that Playboys YETI video that here was my chance to finally understand why I spent all those days throwing a ball against a wall in the heat. Why Selber and I read about the game and sought its deeper meanings. How we knew about Cool Papa Bell when no one else cared. Why Spark and I talked late into the night about watching daytime playoff games at Riverfront

Stadium and Three Rivers. Why the image of Joe Dunnigan standing on the mound continues to haunt my fevered dreams in the thick of the night. Why Elliott and I sought to recapture the magic of that time, but in a new light that shines from the same sun that burned back then. I guess that was another point of discovery, having to go into the wilderness to find my way home.

As for the team's journey, Elliott and I are still in charge, although we are beginning to dole out some off-the-field duties to others. We don't know what may happen to the squad in the future, but I am confident it will be led by stand-up people. We welcome anyone who wants to join on this magical ride as the Moontowers shine their light wherever they are. Keep an eye out, we may be coming to your town one day. And if you are ever driving around Austin at night, glance up at the sky; you may see an actual moontower lighting your way.

As we wrote on our website:

Welcome to Moontowers baseball.

We hope you enjoy the show.

. . . and yes, I still wear sweatpants under my uniform. And is it ever hot!

Visit us and follow the fun at:

www.moontowers.co/

www.instagram.com/austinmoontowers/

ACKNOWLEDGMENTS

I could not have made this trip around the bases without the help of numerous people, beginning with my wife, Liz. Thank you for reading the early drafts (over and over) and never failing to let me know I could do this. You were as important to this project as me. Thank you so much for helping me put the ball in play.

Thank you to my son Andrew. Your enthusiasm for wanting to help create the Moontowers' look back when the team was nothing more than an idea told me this endeavor could be something great!

Thank you to my son Alex, always hustling behind the plate in hundred-degree weather. Your play is greatly appreciated not only as a father, coach, and teammate but also to remind me of how much I loved to play when it was hot outside and I was still young and healthy.

I thank my parents, for showing me how to live a rewarding life and staying true to the people who matter most.

My brother, Mark, thank you for being my first inspiration in the game.

I thank all my cousins in San Antonio who threw the ball with me in backyards and alleyways, especially Ted who played "Hotbox" with me for days on end.

Thank you to all my extended family in Texas and North Carolina. You are guideposts to a way of life I can be proud of.

I especially want to thank my good friend Elliott Hill, who kick-started this journey with the Moontowers one night when he showed me a video about sandlot baseball and asked if I wanted to play again. It was his idea that inspired this story, and nothing has been the same in my life since. I am grateful for half a century of friendship and look forward to all the great things we will still do together.

As for the team, I thank each and every one of you for coming along on the journey . . . you know who you are. (If not, read the book! Ha!) Thank you for believing in Elliott and me and taking a chance on us. Your stories made this special, and I hope I captured what you brought to the team and to my life.

Thank you to our fans who have supported the team and helped us grow. Thank you to our team "moms" for coming out in the heat, the cold, and the rain, sitting in tents and selling merchandise, shouting our names when we are at bat, and being the backbone of the team.

I am grateful to all of my friends who read the early drafts and provided guidance and honest feedback, especially Kerri Monroe, Doug Dickerson, and Jill Gregston (the first person outside of my immediate circle of friends to read it). Thank you for telling me what was good and what wasn't. All of you made this story better.

I am thankful for my coaches along the way who taught me so much about baseball, but also about life.

I am forever grateful for Jack Sanders for starting the whole thing. Without you, we'd have no sandlot baseball at all.

Thank you to Howard Carey who took us under his wing and showed us the ropes and inspired (no, forced) us to create our own team!

Thank you to all of our sandlot opponents—Nic Fowler, Mark Champion, Bryan Hood, Northcutt, Wes Paparone, and all the guys in the Austin sandlot league. Thank you to the Tulsa teams and the Sheeple in Dallas, Ben of the Nashville dollys, Nic Parakeets . . . the sandlot list is endless. Also the good folks at RBI, and anyone else I may have forgotten.

Thank you to the following for helping me become a better player: David Salinas, Adam Ortega, Steve Greinert, Rudy Bautista, Richard Torres, Herb Nauert, Joe Dunnigan, Kevin Tuggle, Gerald Neely, Val Gonzalez, Spark Sheeran, Gerald Wright, and Jim Hector.

I thank Greg "Sucker-Boy" Selber, my baseball twin when we were young. I'm lucky that someone else on this earth enjoyed baseball as much as I did, although we probably shouldn't have read *Ball Four* at such a young age. Thank you for the feedback on this book and your lifelong friendship. We gotta get together!

Thank you to Jay Plotkin. I appreciate your notes and helping the story have more flow. You moved me from first base to second.

Big shout-out to Amy Jo Martin! Thank you for introductions to so many in the literary world, and for giving me enough confidence to really believe in myself and start to think what might happen once I actually finished! You got me around second base heading for third.

A huge thanks to Melanie Saxton, my editor, who waved me around third base and guided me into the plate. I wouldn't have ever made it home without your help.

Thank you to Jason Katzman, Ken Samelson, and the gang at Skyhorse Publishing who saw something in this story and believed it had a place in the world.

Finally, an overwhelming heartfelt thanks to my agent Nena Madonia Oshman, who believed in this story, believed in me (when I didn't think I could see it through), showed me how to keep going and keep believing, and put me in the right hands to get me to the final finish line.

I hope this story inspires anyone who wants to play baseball again on a sandlot with friends and family. Go out and give it a try! It'll be worth it.

ABOUT THE AUTHOR

James "Jim" Matthews is a lifelong fan of baseball, which segued into a career as a TV sports anchor, journalist, filmmaker, public relations professional, small business owner, lawyer, co-creator of the Austin Moontowers sandlot baseball team, and now an author.

Jim grew up in Austin and attended the University of Texas where he received a journalism degree. From there he began an award-winning career as a television sports anchor in California and Texas, including KXAN-TV in Austin from 1996 to 2000. After leaving television, he worked as a media director for Ketchum Public Relations and trained top corporate executives for Fortune 500 companies.

In 2004, he founded Slipstream Films, a full-service production studio producing documentaries, corporate videos, television commercials, and reality shows, working with notable clients such as Nokia, New Balance, and Paula Abdul.

Jim also taught journalism for the American Forces Television Network and graduated magna cum laude from St. Mary's University School of Law in San Antonio. He has been licensed by the Supreme Court of the State of Texas since 2013.

SHINE THE LIGHT

Jim is married with two sons. Besides baseball he enjoys playing golf and the piano, going to concerts, and watching University of Texas sports and the Chicago Cubs.